## MORE PRAISE FOR ED SMITH

Ed Smith's column has been one of the most popular features of the *Pen* since he first started writing the column in 1985. His combination of razor-sharp wit, thoughtful commentary and humour laced with satire has generated a huge following among our readers. His longevity as a columnist is a marvel in itself, but his ability to bounce back from a serious injury and pick up where he left is even more incredible in the eyes of his readers.

ALLAN BOCK, EDITOR
*NORTHERN PEN*

Religion, politics, sex, pop culture, the fishery, family life, or politics—no matter the subject Ed Smith always serves a delicious gutful of social commentary flavoured with his unique blend of wit and humour to put a thought-provoking spin on our world.

RANDY EDISON
*THE NOR'WESTER*

# YOU MIGHT AS WELL LAUGH

# ED SMITH

Flanker Press
St. John's, NL
2004

**Library and Archives Canada Cataloguing in Publication**

Smith, Ed, 1940-
  You might as well laugh / Ed Smith.

ISBN 1-894463-47-1

1. Canadian wit and humor (English) I. Title.

PS8587.M5268Y68 2004          C818'.5402          C2004-901758-6

**PRINTED IN CANADA**

FLANKER PRESS LTD.
P.O. BOX 2522, STATION C
ST. JOHN'S, NL CANADA A1C 6K1
TOLL FREE: 1-866-739-4420
TELEPHONE: (709) 739-4477
FAX: (709) 739-4420
INFO@FLANKERPRESS.COM
WWW.FLANKERPRESS.COM

Canada

We acknowledge the financial support of the Government of Canada through the Book Publishing Industry Development Program (BPIDP) for our publishing program.

We also acknowledge financial assistance from the Government of Newfoundland and Labrador for marketing initiatives.

# CONTENTS

# INTRODUCTION

This is the fifth book of "The View From Here" columns, just in case you want to make your collection complete. I don't know if they've gotten better or worse. If after sampling this you want your money back contact the publisher. I have no intention of refunding anything to anyone.

These columns are from the period 1990 to 1995. Some 250 columns were published during that time. The 75 included here are supposed to be the best of those. Some of them undoubtedly are. Some of them, on the other hand, are, well, you know ...

I do hope you enjoy most of the various epistles contained herein. There is no worse feeling than the conviction you've wasted your money. If such is the case, my suggestion is that you give the book to someone for Christmas, pointing out that it's Newfoundland literature and therefore should be supported. No one ever reads anything given to them for Christmas, anyway. It's against all moral law.

My thanks, as always, to my wife and youngest daughter for their editing and general advice. If this is readable it's largely due to them.

Dedicated to the memory of my father

Alex A. Smith

1916-2002

# Messages From Beyond

This writing of columns is a dangerous business. Every week you lay yourself on the line, vulnerable, defenceless and open to the slings and arrows of outrageous readers. Columnists know that and accept it. It's part of the fun. But sometimes it gets downright scary.

Many people, despite my best efforts, seem to be looking for a serious message in the things I write. Which is fair enough, I guess. The scary bit is that some people are finding it.

Someone will call or write or say in passing, "Really liked the message in your last column!"

And I'll say, "Thank you so much, really. I'm delighted!" Which I am. I'm always delighted when people mention the column without spitting in my face. It means they're reading it, which means my readership should soon be approaching the baker's dozen mark, which will greatly please the editors who are locked into a ten-year multi-million-dollar contract with me.

But the message in the last column? What column was that? I ponder inwardly while smiling outwardly. Oh yes. The one on the significance of buttock freckles in post-puberty Kalahari Bushmen. Okay, the message in that one. Right. What the hell was the message in that?

So I murmur something intelligent like, "Yes, if it concerns the Bushmen it should concern us all," and dash off home (not during work hours, of course) to read the thing again to see what it was I said.

A brief glance through my last literary masterpiece confirms what I already suspected. Nothing even remotely resembling a message. Not even a message to the Bushpersons of the Kalahari.

So what is this? The chap concerned is an intelligent and insightful fellow. If he saw a message in my column there's a message in my column. Somewhere.

Ah, Other Half. She'll know. She picks up on the blaggart, the double entendres, the sexist and the nonsensical. No doubt she saw the message in last week's piece. So I approach her.

"Do you recall last week's column?"

"No."

"You know, the one about freckles and backsides?"

"Oh yes. Not one of my favourites. You sort of reached bottom on that one." Chuckle chuckle.

"Okay, but can you tell me what the message of that column was, as you saw it at the time?"

When OH laughs hard her eyes have a tendency to water. After she stopped wiping them with the better part of a roll of toilet paper, she attempted to speak.

"Message?"

"Yes. The message in that column. What was it?"

Number One Son had to run for another roll of paper. When he got back OH was able to speak again.

"Where on earth do you get the idea there's a message in that absolute nonsense?" A bit strong, perhaps, but fair.

"Well, such-and-such told me today he really enjoyed the message in the last column."

"Really?" New interest here. "You sure he wasn't reading Erma Bombeck? Let me have another look at that. Message, eh? Must be here somewhere."

"That's what I thought."

Moments pass.

"Let's face it, Ed. You're talking about African bums and the related lack of freckles and what that means in terms of global warming. Are you sure he said 'message'? Perhaps he said 'massage.' Do you know him very well?"

"Cut that out! He said 'message.'"

"Okay, but I can't see it. So what's the problem, anyway?"

Problem? She doesn't know the problem? Great God from Gander Bay!

"The problem is that I have obviously said something meaningful and I haven't the slightest idea what it is. I have evidently taken a position and I don't know whose side I'm on. I could be supporting the right of rabbits to a snare-free environment. I could be soliciting missionaries for the Church of the Woolly Haired Sacrificial Lambs, Kalahari Chapter. I could be supporting a financial drive to purchase a bullhorn for Sheila Copps. Who knows what I've said?"

"Those who got the message," said OH under her breath, reaching for the toilet paper again.

"Laugh if you will, but this is serious stuff. It's one thing to defend yourself when you know what you've said. It's quite another to have to stick to your guns when you don't know what you've been firing. This could be my ruination."

"Oh," said OH, "I don't know. Happens to Shakespeare all the time."

"It does?"

"Sure. You think Willy-boy actually meant to say everything college professors think he said? Not a chance. But it's like the Bible. You can read into it anything you want. That's what people are doing with you. They're seeing things you never knew you put there. It's a mark of literary genius."

"It is? You really think so?"

"Of course I do. The Bible and Shakespeare and Ed Smith. Rob, get me some more toilet paper quick."

I don't get no respect.

## The Simple Life

We left home the other day without my toiletries.

OH wasn't too concerned about it. It wasn't her shaving gear. But the solution seemed simple enough. Buy the stuff when we get to Truro, she said. No problem.

The aftershave, the lather and the razors were simple. I'm a combination Aqua Velva, Gillette Foamy and Bic Disposable man. But the toothbrush was a bit more complicated. I discovered the country is overrun with leading dentists, all of whom have lovingly and enthusiastically endorsed each of the four hundred different choices available.

There were hard, soft and medium. There were brushes with little flexible things in the handles and brushes with bristles shaped like the waves of the sea. There were brushes angled to get at the inside of your teeth or angled to reach the downside of your gums. There were brushes to brush nothing but your gums, something I couldn't see the need for since I'd never seen anyone's gums fall out.

But I was impressed with how far technology had come in trying to keep our teeth in our heads instead of in a glass on the night table, and after studying the various shapes and sizes of toothbrushes for some time, I finally decided on a red one.

OH suggested that since we were in this nice little mall I really should get a new pair of jeans. I hate buying anything, except cars and boats, so I didn't think so. She pointed out right in front of half the population of the Maritime Provinces the large red stain decorating the back pocket of the pair I had on.

Thing is, I love that stain. You wouldn't believe the number of women who tell me that I have something on the seat of my pants and then pat the exact spot to emphasize the point. Strangely enough, however, I lost the argument.

Into this clothing store we went to buy jeans. The clerk was a nice young man named Albert who nodded wisely when I said all I wanted was a pair of jeans, size such-and-such, and if he'd get them for me I'd be on my way. He took out a notebook, picked up a pen and said he had a question or two.

"Right," I said, "the inseam is ..."

"No," said Albert, "I need to know if you want Easifit, Slimfit or Relaxedfit."

"Relaxedfit," OH interrupted before I could say Slimfit.

"That's what I thought," said Albert, instantly endearing himself to me. "Now, will that be pleated or non-pleated?"

Pleated? I thought pleats were for skirts and kilts.

"Non-pleated," I said. Albert seemed disappointed, but carried on bravely.

"You have a choice of loose or tapered thigh," he said.

I was beginning to wish myself back at the toothbrush counter.

"What's the difference?" I asked.

"One is tapered," he replied patiently, "and the other is loose."

OH is always the first to pick up the first indications of major irritation on my part and cut in quickly.

"I think you're a loose thigh man, dear," she said. Albert made a note.

"Would he be interested in front scoop pockets?"

OH didn't think so. Neither did Ed and said so strongly.

Albert had obviously decided that where jeans were concerned, and possibly civilization as well, I was a living
Neanderthal and had begun addressing himself to OH. He had
no idea how much that infuriated me, but OH did and looked
decidedly worried.

"Buttons or zipper?"

Buttons? They were selling pants with buttons in the fly? OH
explained, since Albert and I were no longer on speaking terms,
that buttons were the "in" thing. I remembered back to when buttons were the only thing and how much trouble they were and
said flatly, "Tell him zipper."

Albert turned over the third page of his notebook.

"Now," I said to OH, "could you tell him to go get the damn
jeans?" Albert ignored me.

"He'll probably want the antique wash," he said pointedly.

I took a step forward, but OH again intervened and said the
normal wash would be fine.

"Coloured or non-coloured?" he asked without looking up.

"I'm non-coloured," I said. "What's that got to do—?"

"He means the jeans," said OH, as Albert mentally moved me
up a few branches on the *Homo sapiens* family tree.

"I knew that," I replied. "You think I'm stun?"

"We also have the Urban Boot style and the Urban Classic,"
said Albert sweetly, again to OH, "but I don't think he'd be interested in either of those, do you?"

OH looked at me with some alarm, but Albert went blissfully
and ignorantly on.

"He seems to me to be the Eurofit type."

"What's that?"

"Low on the hip, loose in the seat with a straight leg."

OH clutched at my arm.

"He's still talking about jeans," she said gently. "He's not describing you."

But I had had enough.

"Look, Albert, all I want is to buy an honest-to-God pair of jeans without someone getting hurt in the process. Do you think we could manage that?"

Albert looked a bit startled, but thought we might. Off he went. In a moment he was back with something that looked vaguely familiar.

"These are Levis original jeans," he said. "Perhaps this is what you need."

"Okay, start describing these things to me."

"It's all written on the label."

Sure enough, there it was, straightforward and clear: "Sewed with strong thread."

I bought two pairs.

## Letter Perfect

I've been getting anonymous letters.

That in itself isn't so strange. I get thousands of letters every month. Would you believe hundreds? Dozens? How about two postcards and a note slipped under the porch door?

Did you know, incidentally, where the word "anonymous" comes from? Thought not. Okay, call in the kids, wake up grandpa, turn off the TV and prepare to be enlightened.

In a place called "The Watercastle" in Budapest there is a statue to a chap named "Anonymous." He was a scribe to one of Hungary's ancient kings, and was the first to record events in that part of the world in writing. The figure is hooded so that the face is hidden. None of his writings are signed so no one knows his actual identity. He is called simply "Anonymous." Hence, writing that is unsigned, or the author of which is unknown, has come to be called anonymous.

Aren't you glad you read this column? Do you learn stuff like this in the *Globe and Mail?* The *National Post?* *Open Line?* Not hardly.

Anonymous letters to yours truly have been on the increase lately. And not one of them has contained money or an offer of marriage. Not that they're all critical or negative. One had several suggestions for stories to use in the column. After reading them, I can see why the sender didn't want to sign his or her name. I'm no prude myself, Lord knows, but some of my editors just don't get off on that sort of thing. Anyway, this is a person who can have a lot of fun just sitting around thinking.

The anonymous authors of my letters seem to be more interested in making statements than in seeking answers. Could be politicians. But since I can't respond to them directly, I thought it might be fun, just for once, to answer some of their questions and comments right here in the column. You may not agree. Poof on you. Here they are anyway, prioritized in order of importance.

"What makes you think you're so ****hot?"

The four stars stand for four letters, the first of which is *S* and the last of which is *T*. The word "manure" may be substituted but it doesn't have the same impact. Still, it's a valid question. All I need now is a valid answer, which doesn't come easy. The question is incomplete. As ****hot as what? As a budget forecaster for the provincial government? As a statistician for the federal Department of Fisheries? As a one-legged acrobat with the palsy walking a tightrope across the St. John's Narrows in a Northeaster? As any St. John's city councillor? What? Until I have a basis for comparison, you see, it is difficult to estimate just how ****hot I really am.

"Why don't you just quit and get it over with?" Truth is, I've been trying to, but it ain't easy. I've even tried a variation of the patch. You know how the patch works to help people stop smoking? It releases a little bit of nicotine into the body to help wean the smoker off the drug. Well, I tried the same idea to quit column writing. I taped one of the cheques from the publishers of this marvellous paper to my bankbook, but it didn't work. I found I needed the money more than ever, so I'm still writing. Perhaps some day ... In the meantime, I don't write in the presence of my family. Second-hand satire isn't good for anyone.

"How come a supposedly highly educated person such as yourself does not know the difference between the words 'compliment' and 'complement'?"

Now that one really stung because I do. Prove it? Of course. "The daily complement of compliments around here is not that high." Okay? I don't know in which publication "compliment" was printed for "complement." I don't see them all, you know. And again I don't know where the complainer is from. But I checked the original that goes out from this office and on that "complement" was spelled c-o-m-p-l-e-m-e-n-t the way it's supposed to be, and not c-o-m-p-l-i-m-e-n-t the way it isn't supposed to be.

Sooooo, much as I hate to say it, someone in the office of the paper concerned decided I didn't know what I was doing and changed it. Happens all the time. And it makes me furious. So do me an enormous favour, won't you, and call them and tell them off about it. You have my permission to do it anonymously.

"Just what do you believe in, anyway?"

The best answer I ever heard to that one was given by Kevin Costner in *Bull Durham*. Among other things, "I believe in long, slow, wet kisses that last three days (I can't hold my breath that long), in opening presents Christmas Day instead of Christmas Eve (same here), and that Lee Harvey Oswald acted alone (I just watched *JFK* and it seems Costner has changed his mind on that one)."

What do I believe? I believe that the pen is mightier than the sword, that love is mightier than hate and that the Toronto Maple Leafs are mightier than the Montreal Canadiens. I believe in warm beds and cold beer. I believe in God. I believe that what goes around comes around. And I believe that anonymous letter-writers will roast in everlasting flames.

I know this sounds tacky, but I'd like to thank those of you who sent me Christmas cards. You're both wonderful people. In fact, and I can never say it enough, I appreciate all your letters. My New Year's resolution is to catch up on my mail and answer each of you warmly and personally.

That, and never to try singing opera underwater.

## Parenthood

OH and I have decided not to have any more children. After thirty years of marriage we feel capable of making that kind of decision. We thought about it, talked it out, cried a bit, discussed it with our minister and then said the hell with it. We're simply not going through that again.

Every once in awhile, you'll hear some simple naive soul talking about the sheer horror of raising two kids under six.

"Can't be up to them, my dear. Under your feet all the time, messing their nappies, getting grass stains ingrained on their little backsides. Throwing tantrums. How does one survive this at all?"

I'll tell you. You survive it by talking to someone who has children in their late teens and older, and then falling on your knees in humble gratitude to the Creator for small mercies, no matter how dirty and stinky the small mercies might be.

The terrible twos? The terrible twos are only terrible when one hasn't lived through the terrible twenties. Skinned knees and chipped teeth are only a problem for those who haven't survived smashed love affairs and bruised egos. Back-answering and saucy tongues are only irritating when you haven't experienced the joy of knowing that the fruits of your union consider you to be an unadulterated jackass, which they do for most of their early adult years.

Unless you have raised at least two offspring to marriageable age, you can't talk about raising children, at least not in my presence and not with any authority. The real fun only begins when they're into their early teens and lasts well into the age of consent, whatever that is.

Compare the problem of having an infant spit up in your face with the horror of seeing your seventeen-year-old daughter taking up with someone like Rex Murphy. In the former case, you wipe it off, swear on the kid (it doesn't understand a word you say, anyway) and carry on pushing the strained peas down its greedy little gullet and out into its diaper.

Seventeen years later, all you can do is sit home alone, watch the clock as it creeps past midnight and caress your twelve-gauge, double-barrel, semi-automatic Savage shotgun. You can also reflect on precisely where you intend to put the first load of shot when the young bugger who's kept her out this late turns up on your doorstep.

I had a call not long ago from a frantic father whose young daughter had taken up with an older Lothario with a reputation for lovin' and leavin' 'em pregnant.

"You've raised three," he said, "so tell me what I can do. You must have an answer for this one."

I did. In fact, I had two alternatives for him. The first and most preferable was to do nothing, except hope she's got sense enough to see what's happening sooner rather than later and gets herself out of it. You trying to stop her, I advised, will only make it worse.

"But I can't sit and do nothing," he protested. "I'm going crazy just thinking about it. There must be something I can do."

"Yes," I said, "there's my second alternative. You can kill him."

Happily, he called back sometime later to say that his daughter had, like the prodigal son, come to herself. But do you have any idea what that man went through? You don't? Then shut up about the problems of raising kids. Do you know the sheer joy of having three children yelling and screaming in your living room over the TV remote control? You don't see the joy in it? Yep, you're a younger parent, all right. The joy, you ninny, is in knowing exactly where they are at that very moment.

Consider having your very young daughter set out to drive across the continental US of A in the dead of winter in a vehicle not expected to get past Corner Brook on a summer's day. Consider not hearing from her for two or three days as she wends her carefree way between Boston and Pittsburgh. Consider your feelings as you watch the latest Detroit news with the latest muggings, carjackings, kidnappings and other sundry crimes not listed in Leviticus and guaranteed to drive a father clean out of his mind. And lastly, consider how quickly that father would swap places with the chap who's lying awake half the night listening to the screams of a youngster who's cutting teeth.

I know you think life is tough when your five-year-old busts into the bedroom just as firecrackers are going off and bells are ringing and for one fleeting moment you see clearly why you wanted to get married in the first place. His eyes are wide and his mouth is open and he's chock full of questions about what he's just seen mommy and daddy doing. I agree. It's no fun trying to explain that sort of thing to yourself, let alone a youngster.

But you do not know the meaning of real torment until your eighteen-year-old walks in at the moment of truth and busts out in raucous laughter. Granted, no explanations from you are needed at this age, and no apologies necessary from anyone. Just absolute total mortification and shame for you and your partner for life in sickness and in health, and a desire to return immediately to the dust from whence you sprung.

No, the infant years aren't the reason we decided to give up childbearing. Those are relatively peaceful and good. It's when they're "grown" that the crises just keep coming and coming. In fact, my young friends, when we old-timers hear you talking about your problems with your little toddlers, there's only one thing that makes us tolerate you at all.

The sure and certain knowledge that your turn is coming.

## Time for Families

"If the Spirit moves me."

That's what Father said when I asked him if he and Mother were coming for Christmas this year.

Father and the Spirit have a very close relationship. In situations where he is not entirely sure what he wants to do, Father will invariably fall back on the Spirit for moral support and guidance.

The interesting thing is that I have never known the Spirit to move Father to do something he doesn't want to do. When the Spirit finally decides to act, you can be sure that Father has already made the decision to do precisely what the Spirit is now moving him to do.

Still, one never knows what the current situation might be, so I asked my mother if she knew the state of the relationship between Father and the Spirit these days.

"Pretty good as far as I know," she said. "Yesterday the Spirit moved him to saw up half a cord of wood in the driving rain with an electric chainsaw."

Mother's tone suggested that she was somewhat out of sync with both man and spirit, and not for the first time.

We also invited Other Half's father down from Toronto to spend the holidays with us, but he declined without aid of the Spirit. He's got two sisters in Toronto, and between the three of them they share a total of two hundred and seventy-seven years of living.

My own feeling is that his girlfriend has at least as much to do with the decision as his sisters. She has no intention of making the rounds of the Toronto Christmas parties by herself.

Daughter Number One is the first of the offspring to arrive. Daughter, however, has two little problems, each equipped with digestive tracts and plumbing. We also have two little problems of the same kind. Two dogs plus two dogs equals four mouths and four sprinkler systems, which does nothing for Other Half's bad attitude towards math.

Anyway, Daughter asked in advance about bringing them home for Christmas, and Other Half made comments which would not win her the SPCA seal of approval. They wouldn't help her chances much at the Pearly Gates, either.

I think they finally compromised. Daughter could come home if the dogs didn't.

Daughter Number Two is on Fogo Island, earning money on a regular and permanent basis which is a blessing right up there with having your own winery. In her view, Fogo Island lies somewhere between Paradise and Shangri-La. We're all mildly surprised that she's managed to tear herself away to spend a few days with her aged parents.

If we hadn't lived for a year on Fogo Island ourselves, back when we were not much older than she, we'd never understand it. The Island has its own beauty, but it is not Bermuda for climate, British Columbia for trees or West Germany for highways. There isn't a big market for surfboards.

But when they talk about Newfoundland hospitality and warmth, the essence of it is found there. No one escapes being captivated by the charm of the Fogo Islanders and Daughter, like her parents, is no exception.

She's home for the holidays, but we know that on her way back to the Island she'll be singing. And as far as we know it will have nothing to do with men. For a change.

Daughter Number Three flies into Deer Lake from Boston. From here to Deer Lake and back is two hundred and forty kilometres through barren wilderness. In order to get even for all the nasty things I've ever said about flying, the airline is getting her in at midnight—the night of our office party.

They do it every year. And they make sure there's a blizzard raging to give the trip that extra little something. I'm the only one who notices such details, of course. Not having seen each other since August, Mother and Daughter manage to find a few things to talk about on the way home. I find comfort in the fact that this particular conversation isn't costing me long distance rates.

Number One Son, like the Prodigal Son's brother, we have with us always or for one more year, whichever comes first.

We were talking to friends the other day whose children are grown and gone, much like our own. We asked about them as we always do. Where are they now? How are they doing? Are they coming home for Christmas?

"No," our friend said, somewhat wistfully. "No one coming home this year."

I know how close they are as a family, again like ourselves, and I started thinking about what our Christmas might be like if dogs and Fogo took preference over coming home, if planes didn't fly at midnight and if the Spirit and Father had a falling out.

Christmas is for children, the old song says, and that's true because at Christmas we're all children. The wonder and magic of childhood and the wonder and magic of Christmas are the same.

But even more, Christmas is for families. We're fortunate enough to be together for the most part this year, and we'll savour that closeness and warmth for one more time and be grateful.

We wish as much for you.

# A Methodology for Skinning Cats

There's more than one way to skin a cat.

Why anyone would want to is beyond me, but if you are so inclined there's evidently more than one way to do it.

While skinning cats isn't that common anymore, some people have obviously done it, found that there are options and generalized accordingly. Perhaps there was a time when skinning cats was fairly commonplace among our ancestors. I really couldn't say why. Perhaps they simply didn't like cats. Perhaps they hated cats. Some people do.

Thing is, if cat-skinning wasn't popular at some point in our history where did the saying come from? Why isn't it "there's more than one way to skin a moose"? Or a fox? Or a seal? Nope, cats they said and cats they meant. I refuse to pursue the matter further at this time.

I haven't skinned many cats myself, but as a long-time big-game hunter, I have skinned enough rabbits to consider myself a bit of an expert on the subject. Speaking of subjects, skinning animals is not the subject of this week's column, but since the topic's come up we may as well say a word or two about it. We'll get to the keynote theme momentarily.

A few pointers on skinning do seem to be in order, given it's a practice that goes on all around us on a continuing basis. Cows get skinned before they become rump roasts at the supermarket. Sheep are skinned—thank God!—before they get served with mint jelly. And fish are skinned before they become fillets.

Man, as George Bernard Shaw observed, is the only animal that can be skinned twice. You may not have spent much time pondering these truths, but truths they are. Anyway, please be aware that the language used in the following paragraphs may be offensive to some, particularly those who have an extreme fondness for our furry friends and are particularly sensitive about separating them from their hides.

I give that warning because the last time I said something mildly unkind about pussycats, a dear lady wrote to give me a piece of her mind. She included in the letter a photo of one of her cats. Then she said she hoped I'd burn in hell. The picture is still on the wall above my desk within easy reach. So if I go, Ma'am, you should know the cat is going with me. At any rate, consider yourselves warned.

First, it helps immensely in skinning any animal for it to be dead. This would be especially true for cats. Indeed, in that case it is better for both the skinner and the skinnee if one of them is a corpse. Just as an aside, the Inuit prefer to skin their animals gut-in. I myself fancy the gut-out technique. There are pros and cons, as you probably know. It depends on the type of animal and your situation at the time.

Again, while not wishing to get too graphic, one assumes one could begin skinning from either end of the animal, or perhaps even in the middle. As an expert, I would not recommend the latter, although no true hunter would get too dogmatic about it. In stating that there is more than one way to skin a cat, therefore, one must allow for flexibility and personal preference.

Actually, the statement concerning the multiplicity of cat-skinning techniques has nothing to do with the explicit act of defrocking felines. It suggests that there's more than one way to do anything, which leads us to today's topic.

I was reminded of the cat-skinning declaration while reading about this US Air Force officer who was court-martialled a little while ago for chasing a buxom (are we allowed to say "buxom" anymore? It's so difficult to keep up with these things) secretary around his office. Sufficient to say, neither officer nor secretary needed further skinning. Both were buck-naked at the time.

His superiors felt that running around his office in his birthday suit with a young lady whose birthday must have been on the same day seemed somehow inappropriate for an officer of the US Air Force. Some Air Force brass felt strongly it was downright un-American and demanded that he be charged with ... well, something. And that was the problem. With what offence could they indict this officer? The young lady was of consenting age and consenting disposition. The officer hadn't left his office so there was no question of neglect of duty or abandoning his post.

So the lawyers searched and searched and finally found the long-sought-for regulation that had been so flagrantly violated. They charged the officer with being out of uniform while on the job and were properly pleased with themselves. More than one way to skin a cat, they were reported as saying. Can't get him for one thing get him for something else. Case closed, right?

Well, not quite. The officer in question was familiar with the skinning cats axiom himself, it seems. Although he was as guilty as he had been naked, he hired a lawyer to get him out of this mess without further damage to his career. The lawyer searched the Air Force regulations diligently and suddenly there it was, the regulation that would—and did—get his client acquitted and returned to his desk.

"An officer shall not be considered to be out of uniform if he is suitably attired for the sport in which he is engaged."

Meow.

## Potpourri

Hi! I'm in the Bosting States.

You've never heard of the Bosting States?

Neither had I until a lady of our acquaintance from one of the more remote corners of the province, shall we say, went up to Boston many years ago to spend the winter with her aunt. She returned the following spring, having put on a few airs and a rather queer (used in the traditional sense) accent, and let it be known to whomever would listen that she had been to "the Bosting States."

That's where I am this week, visiting Daughter Number Three who goes to school in Boston. I'm telling you so you'll miss me. How could you miss me if you didn't know I was gone? Right.

But in the meantime let me explain something to you.

This delightful and entertaining column is written primarily to give the reader a chuckle. You understand? Ha ha and ho ho and all that. I am aware that at times my efforts may result in nothing more than a ho hum smile, or worse. But I have hopes that at other times some of you may actually laugh right out loud, with feeling. Whether with me or at me is unimportant.

It's like going to church. The idea is that you should feel better when you finish than when you started. There are those among you who may feel that comparing this column to the act of worship is somewhat blasphemous, and of such I beg forgiveness, although not very hard. Divine inspiration may be at work here, too, you know.

Ninety-five per cent of what I write, therefore, should not be taken seriously. The other five per cent should be ignored. Some readers tend to ignore more than five per cent but that's a matter of personal choice.

Whyfore are we talking about this? Let me tell you.

You may recall a column awhile ago which talked about Newfoundland getting out of Canada while the going is good. How Ottawa treats us like political lepers. Me forming the Society of Secessionists (SOS). Right, that's the one.

Well, my dear, in the days and weeks following that particular little article I had (a) offers to join secret separatist groups, both local and national—not a word of a lie; (b) offers to join the SOS as soon as I got it going; (c) offers of cohabitation with members of the opposite sex; and (d) offers to support me if I wanted to run for president of the Fisherpersons' Union. The last came from Smilin' Earle McCurdy.

Well, not really, but in all truth I did get letters from Ontario down that took my "separatist" ideas quite literally and quite seriously, and that's no laughing matter.

I have to admit that particular column was one of those rare occasions on which genuine feeling tends to show through the brilliant wit and satire. Most of the time I keep my real thoughts to myself—in the name of common decency, if nothing else. But I do have a great depth of feeling over what is happening to our province and our country, and I guess that day it showed.

The whole fisheries fiasco makes me sick and angry at the same time. And I do blame the federal government for the whole mess, and I really don't think they care one way or the other up there. And when Richard Cashin gets so frustrated and upset that cussing on the beggars is the only thing that will give him any relief at all, I'm right there with him, body and soul.

But I have absolutely no desire to see Newfoundland and Labrador taken out of Canada's political bosom, at least not at the moment, and to seriously propose otherwise is totally irresponsible. My purpose in mentioning the idea at all was to make the point in an exaggerated fashion, as is my style, that Ottawa's treatment of us is the sort of thing that could drive us in that direction. But it's not a direction I personally would want to take.

Besides, any organization called SOS would be in danger of being mistaken for a soap pad.

Neither am I anti-Quebec. I am against those things that divide us (the only two exceptions being gender and the Gulf of St. Lawrence), such as political borders and denominational lines. And I'm for those things that bind us together, such as federalism and our common admiration of Joe Clark.

Mulroney's bosom is another thing altogether, and being torn from it would not cause me real pain. That leaves us in the bosom of either the NDP lady leader or the new Liberal gentleman leader, and while I'm quite prepared to consider being attached to the former, I would rather not consider the latter option at this time.

I mean really, do you have any desire to be drawn to any part of Jean Chrétien, let alone his bosom? You may want to think further about it.

One more thing: frequently, people will write or call asking me to pick up the cudgels on behalf of some serious and worthy local charity, such as the editors of the student newspaper at Memorial.

I am really sorry, but I don't do that sort of thing. I get paid to make people laugh, not think. Okay, so I get paid too much.

Love you, too. But from now on call Geoffrey Simpson or Oprah with your causes, will you? They're much more serious and passionate than I and would do almost as good a job.

Almost, I said.

## Uncommon Sense

We have sensible children.

Modesty be darned, we have really sensible children. When you've just had ample proof that your offspring are practically without fault, there's a need to share the feeling. I know you understand and approve.

Before going further, I should point out what you already know. Sensible for me may be somewhat different from what sensible is for you. You may feel, for example, that Tammy Faye Bakker has a sensible approach to fundraising for the Lord, whereas I'm liable, nay more than liable, to find a few flaws. Or that dining, dancing and etcetering with one's beloved is a sensible way to end the day, whereas I might feel it isn't. I use that last example for the sake of argument only.

A sensible daughter for you may be one who sings in the church choir, dates the local pastor and is always home by nine thirty. And I have to admit that's not half bad if you trust clergymen.

Perhaps the sensible son in your mind has his own car, buys his own gas and pays for his own insurance. This is an extremely rare breed of individual in either gender, but nothing says you can't dream.

Let me tell you what sensible in children is all about.

The other night one of my three girls called home. Calling home, I might add, is not a totally uncommon occurrence. Anytime the phone rings after midnight, neither one of us wants to answer it because we know it means the sky has fallen in on one or more of our offspring. Actually, most of their calls come in at about five minutes before midnight, which is five minutes before the rates are substantially reduced.

Anyway, we got this call from one of them last week. After the initial pleasantries from her mother—"Are you sick? Are you studying? Are you coming home?"—daughter dropped her little bombshell.

"I think you should know, Mom," she began ...

Now this sort of thing scares the living hell out of her father listening in on the extension. Do you have any idea just how many endings such a sentence can have?

"I think you should know, Mom, that ...

... I've been kicked out of university."

... I've been kicked out of St. John's."

... I'm running away to Venice with an Italian named Giovanni."

... I'm dating Rex Murphy."

I know there are parents out there who can empathize with this stuff. Isn't it awful? The functioning universe ceases to breathe as it waits for the next few words.

"I think you should know, Mom," she said, "that I won't be needing any more money this semester."

At that point, you pick yourself up off the floor, lever your jaw back into position and thank God for His tender mercies. She doesn't need any more money until next year. There's a sensible girl, right? But that's not all.

We have another daughter who likes to talk about weddings. Given the fact that it costs almost as much to get married as to get buried, the word "wedding" is right up there with "dismemberment" as one of my all-time favourites. So I try to stay out of those rambling conversations the girls have with their mother about upcoming nuptials. As if I had a choice.

But the other night, almost asleep on the extension, I perked right up. Was I hearing right?

"Actually, Mom," she was saying, "we're thinking we might elope."

Sometimes I wonder what I do to deserve such goodness and thoughtfulness in my children. With that kind of attitude, she'll get nothing but encouragement from her father, I can tell you. Do you begin to see why I'm boasting?!

One more example. One of the major concerns in a father's life is the kind of company his daughter keeps when she's out gallivanting around. If your memory is long enough to remember your own courtship rituals, panic can set in without warning.

But again, my child has achieved commonsense status. At the moment—and I do stress "at the moment"—she's enamoured of a young chap who hails from British Columbia. You see? That's sensible. There's a whole continent between him and her. Actually, the lad is studying in Ontario but I'm still happy with the distance involved. I'll worry about holiday weekends another time.

That leaves Number One Son who is well on the way to becoming sensible in his own right. Take today, for example, when I missed the post he was holding for me and hit him in the head with a five-pound hammer. He let out a most uncharacteristic expletive before slumping to the ground, but he's only fifteen and it was an awful smack.

I made a deal with him then and there that I'd forget what he said if he'd forget that I struck him. In other words, neither of us would say anything to his mother. He agreed, sensible lad, and we'd have shaken on it on the spot except both his hands were being held to his head.

How blessed a thing it is to have sensible children.

Sorry, Mom and Dad.

## Aging With Dignity

"How do you prepare for getting old?"

We were having lunch at a restaurant in the Avalon Mall. Daughter sounded serious, but I didn't look up. Perhaps she was talking to someone else, such as her intended.

"Ah yes," said Intended, with all the wisdom of his twenty-four years, "Getting old must be really scary. How do you get ready for it?"

No one answered. In the silence that followed, I glanced up from my forbidden fruit—cod tongues fried in onions and scrunchions—to see if these were rhetorical questions, or if there was someone around qualified to answer. They were both staring expectantly at me. The implication was clear: I above all people should know.

There is an arrogance in the young that tends to raise my hackles, assuming I still have hackles left. How would I know how one prepares for old age? At my age, it's not something one thinks a lot about. Perhaps I should, but I don't. I'm still trying to burst free of adolescence, according to those who know and love me (not always the same group).

I do admit to being older. I'm older than Michael Jackson. I'm older than Clyde Wells. I'm older than Sheila Copps, I think, which is where this line of thinking abruptly ends. But everyone is older than someone else, and everyone is younger than someone else. Relatively speaking, then, I could be older or younger and so could you.

Aren't you glad you read this column? No big words or anything. Just pure simple logic.

Where was I? Oh yes, old, and how you prepare for it. I finally did some thinking about the problem, and as usual came up with some scintillating answers. And just as usual, I'm willing to share the results of my intellectual findings with the world at large. The following guidelines are taken from my upcoming book *Older and Loving It*, subtitled *What the Hell Choice Have You Got, Anyway?*

In a word, one prepares for getting old the same way one prepares for an argument with one's spouse or a fight with Mike Tyson—one avoids it. Impossible to avoid getting old, you say? Not at all. Allow me to explain how. Rosicrucians, eat your hearts out.

Bottom Line Rule: hide it from everyone. People get old only because other people perceive they are older and treat them that way. Therefore, keep them from finding out. Why do people say stupid, silly things to babies like "itchy kitchie coo" and "goo goo"? Because they perceive that they're talking to babies. If babies could hide the fact that they are babies, they wouldn't have to put up with all that nonsense. Same with getting older.

"I'm with you so far, Eddie," you say admiringly, "but exactly how does one hide getting older?"

I knew we'd get to this point and consequently I am ready. There are several methods from which you may take your pick.

Personally, I find using them all in a kind of combined strategy gives the best results.

First, lie through your dentures. One of the marvellous things about getting older is that one can lie with impunity. People expect it of you. So tell the biggest whoppers you can think of. Even if no one believes you, you'll still get respect. But to be really effective your lying has to be in the right direction. For example, you let something like this drop at a party within earshot of several people.

"Yep, Minnie and I are thinking of buying a new house, closer to an elementary school, you know."

"Margie is beginning to worry about the effect of birth control pills on the body, so the old love life may be curtailed a bit from now on."

This kind of talk is bound to leave a certain impression with those who listen to you.

Second, adopt the language of the younger. This takes some practice but the effort is well worth it.

"Totally awesome tea party, Mildred!"

"This is one cool bingo game, dude!"

"Far out support hose, Eleazor."

People think they can tell a lot about you by the way you talk. So talk the way you want them to see you. Nothing tough about that.

Third, dress younger. Don't go to extremes with this or you'll simply look foolish, and if there's one thing worse than being seen as old, it's being seen as old and foolish. Anyway, calico dresses are out, as are wide ties, slack-arse pants and bandanas. Enough said.

Okay, Eddie, you're saying. That's all well and good. But suppose I'm already past that stage and everyone knows how old I am and people call me "skipper" and "pops" and "nanny" and stuff like that. What do I do now?

Happily, I have the answer.

Don't worry about it. If you need a battery and a pair of booster cables to get you kick-started in the morning, so be it. If your arms aren't long enough to hold the book far enough from your eyes to read it, don't give it a second thought. If you find yourself constantly singing songs like "The Sweet Bye and Bye" and "Beyond the Sunset," put it down to involuntary nerve reflexes.

If you're already old and everyone knows it, don't worry about that, either. That's the second-best advice I can give.

Ah, but Eddie, you say, it's too late for that, too. I'm an older man and I do worry about it. I'm past all those stages and it's too late for your strategies. Is there anything at all for an old fellow like me?

Sure there is, my friend, perhaps the best advice of all.

Run off with a younger woman.

## I'll Fly Away

Let's talk about the universal life force.

Stay with me a moment, now. This isn't as bad as it looks. I refer to that unquenchable essence of life-giving energy which permeates all living things and defies all attempts to destroy or reverse it.

I want to talk about this irresistible life force especially as it applies to houseflies and alders.

We have a little cabin in beautiful St. Patrick's. Lest you think I'm being pretentious, understand that of the three major types of summer dwelling: cabin, cottage and summer home, ours is at the bottom of the status heap.

Your normal cabin is a humble affair consisting mainly of an old stove surrounded by bits of wood and a few logs. Some of your better cabins have indoor toilets. Some simply have large trees in close proximity to the back door.

The cottage is several steps up from the cabin. It usually has a bathroom complete with towels and toilet tissue, and cute little signs that read: "We aim to please; you aim, too, please!" Most of the large trees immediately adjacent to cottages have been cut down because no one has need to disappear behind one now and then. Cottages often have sinks with drains into which you can throw slop water.

The highest form of summer dwelling is your summer home, so called because you can live in it winter or summer. The bathrooms don't even need signs telling you how to flush the toilet properly. Summer homes have brand new mattresses and come complete with electric fly zappers and carpets. Cottages have beds and chesterfields handed down from people who have summer homes. Cabins have only bunks because the furniture is all gone with the kids to university.

In a cabin you never worry about the dirt on your feet when you go inside. In a cottage you have to stomp your boots clean before entering. You're not allowed into a summer home unless you throw away your boots, burn your socks and wash your feet in the River Jordan.

We have a cabin with vague overtones of cottage.

Where were we? Ah yes. The universal life force.

This cabin of ours may not be the equivalent of Donald Trump's summer hideaway, but it is airtight, for the most part. The windows have screens, likewise the doors, and neither the roof nor the floor has any holes that we know about. Each time we leave our little cabin, we spray it with seventeen different kinds of pesticides before closing everything up tight. Cows a quarter of a mile away across the cove have been known to keel over in a coma when downwind of one of our sprayings.

But the very next time we return, even if it's the next day, we are met with roughly fourteen million happy houseflies buzzing merrily through our airspace and obviously disgustingly healthy. I immediately reduce all flies to tiny insect corpses with a makeshift swatter made of three-quarter inch plywood and two-by-four. The whole mess is then shovelled into a stove loaded with creosote logs which tend to cause heat approximating hell's flames.

But the very next day come hell, high water or DDT there they are again by the thousands and laughing in my face. I know it's the same flies because we've tagged a few and traced them through poison, fire and flyswatter back to their home on the window sill.

I am convinced that nothing can kill your standard cabin fly. Accordingly, why are we looking elsewhere for cures for disease and politics? Why does the fountain of youth continue to elude people like Andy Wells? Surely in this day and age it is possible to identify, isolate and reproduce the essence of a fly's being, and have it in pill form before I die of old age.

I have sprayed a clump of alders with stuff that would make Agent Orange look like Kool-Aid; cut it down to the ground and reduced it to sawdust with my trusty chain saw; poured gallons of kerosene oil over it and set it ablaze; and last but not least, had our oldest dog lift his leg against it three times. Once has been known to vulcanize the rubber in a Michelin tire.

Within thirty days, new green alders are guaranteed to be pushing their way up through the scorched and poisoned earth.

Earlier this summer, and this is honest to my Maker, I cut a few alders to serve as poles for my bean plants. I sharpened out the ends to a fine point and drove them into the ground. Within two weeks the alders were sprouting fresh new leaves and growing mad. The beans, watered, fertilized, and lovingly attended, have yet to be seen.

They tell us there's a wood shortage in this province. If we could just find some way to make the alder grow as large as your average black spruce, we'd have to import labour from Ontario to feed our three hundred paper mills and keep the highways clear.

Surely there must be some explanation for this boundless life force. Perhaps it's all psychological. Perhaps the fly and the alder don't know they're supposed to give up and die. Perhaps the human problem is that somebody gave us the option.

Whatever, one other thing is sure besides death and taxes.

Flies, crushed to earth, shall rise again.

## Maritime Diary

We are crossing the great wide Gulf again.

You know the one. The *Caribou*, the *Joseph and Clara* and the inexpensive cafeterias. This makes the third or fourth time this year so far, which is a bit much for someone who would rather clean toilet bowls. But who gets a choice in this life? Not I, said the sparrow.

As with several others aboard This Thing, we're going up to spend Thanksgiving weekend with Number One Son, who's in Mount Allison, and Daughter Number Three, who isn't.

Daughter Number Three has it all over and done with, Magna Cum Laude, mind you, and only an arm and a leg missing from her father. I'm afraid to check any other of my body parts. So is OH, although I've encouraged her to try.

It occurs to us partway across the Gulf that there's something wrong with this picture. Used to be that the kids came home to see us for the holidays. Is it a sign of the times that we're now going to see them? We began to realize we could bring six offspring home for what it's costing us to go in the opposite direction.

So what's it all about, Alfie? Why are we doing this? For the joy of the trip? The joy of a trip across the gulf?! Give me a break! There's more joy in having a boil on your whatsit lanced.

What gulfs between (us) and the seraphim.

That line of Markham's might apply were it not rather difficult to imagine Son as seraphim, or anything else in the angelic realm. Takes after his father (this line inserted at no extra cost by his mother).

I do admit that driving through the Cape Breton countryside at dawn does tend to take the wrinkles from one's soul. The sun is an orange glow behind the hills, and the trees float freely above the mists that are vainly trying to hide from the day in the still-dark valleys. With the first rays of the sun the hillsides come quickly alive with the brazen scarlet of the maples and the new gold of the birches. The waters of the Bras D'Or Lake throw sparkling kisses to the morning, and the sailboats ride softly, gently mating with their other selves on the flat, soft surface.

Lord, that's beautiful.

It is a pure Thanksgiving morning. It's like driving through one of those October calendars. I expect at any moment to go crashing out through the back and into a wall.

And it's a gentle country, so unlike the rugged, harsher terrain of Newfoundland. But I get a sudden insight into what has helped mould the strong individualism of the Newfoundland character. It comes at least in part from the restless energy and the raw strength of the far-from-gentle elements surrounding us. Of course, I could be wrong.

Strange to find ourselves at Mt. Allison thirty years after our student days. Has it changed that much? Not at all. Look, we're still here, walking slowly hand in hand down the grassy slopes toward the Lily Pond. And there we are rushing off to class, late again. Nothing has changed except the names, right? Wrong.

Climbing the stairs to Son's room on the third floor of his residence, I am struck by unfamiliar sights and sounds: the sights and sounds of women. They're everywhere. Women live directly across the hall from him and on all sides of him. Strangely, he doesn't seem to mind. I recall that thirty years ago being caught in a women's residence on that same campus was reason enough for expulsion. However there were always some fools who thought the price was worth it.

OH, before she was OH, was allowed out until ten thirty— midnight on weekends—and to sneak past the reception desk in the porch of her residence was to be struck dead. The only thing that saved our relationship was an old car trained to break down about fifty miles from Sackville about an hour before curfew time. They don't make cars like that anymore.

So what's changed so much in thirty years that male and female, once kept as strictly separate as red roosters and white hens, should now be cooped up in the same henhouse day and night? Have our values changed that much, or our behaviour? Are young men and women more trustworthy now, or more self dis- ciplined? Or just luckier?

For a while, I thought I was born thirty years too soon, but then I remembered how great it used to be, after waiting for her for an hour, to see OH come tripping down those stairs looking like a million dollars. And the sheer magic of hours spent walking by the Lily Pond until her time was up and we dragged ourselves back to her dorm. With women omnipresent I wonder where the magic is. Seems to me to be about the same as being married long before you should be. I wonder what modern fools decided co-ed residences would be worth it.

Anyway, here we all are at OH's sister's house in the Valley. Sister and her husband and their five offspring; OH and me and our two; a friend of one of theirs and a friend of one of ours. How many is that? It's a crowd, and it's a good crowd. We're all having a great time, watching the Jays and renting movies and going to a Frank Mills concert and playing Trivial Pursuit until daylight and watching the Jays and going for scarlet-coloured walks through the trees and watching the Jays.

There are worse ways to spend Thanksgiving.

## Hotelgate

Other Half and I have this interesting lifestyle.

It's not that exciting, as lifestyles of the rich and famous go. We don't fly off to Monte Carlo for the weekend or to the Alps for the ski season. Hugh Hefner and I aren't buddies (sigh), and Princess Di doesn't call OH on her birthday.

When we talk about going south, we mean Marystown to visit Daughter Number One. "Out West" is Corner Brook for a wild weekend at the Glynmill Inn. "Across the pond" means exactly that—worms, fishing pole and the works.

We did fly off to Vancouver for a week three or four years ago, but while we were gone the house next door burned down, the roof practically blew off our house, the greenhouse blew to pieces and the new refrigerator broke down, spoiling a goodly portion of frozen goods. We decided to stick closer to home.

We do, however, have our moments, the stuff memories and divorces are made of. Usually they have to do with my aversion to hotel elevators, or my equal dislike of flying machines and the experiences thereof. The latest had to do with neither.

Last week, OH had to be in St John's a couple of days before I was due myself in the Big Crabapple. My reservation at My Favourite Hotel (MFH) was for Friday night, so I suggested to OH that it might be nice if we could rendezvous at the hotel on Friday afternoon, seeing as how it's only six months to our anniversary and all.

She could go down to MFH and book into my room about midafternoon. If I arrived first, well, I'd already be there, wouldn't I. If one of us had to be late, he or she would leave a message for the other, something like "If I'm not there in an hour start without me." You know how it is with us young folk.

Simple enough arrangement? Certainly.

I got into St. John's town about three on Friday afternoon. OH would no doubt be waiting for me by this time, so I took the shortcut back of the Avalon Mall. Wonder of wonders, the desk clerk at MFH assured me my wife had not arrived and there was no message. Great. Gave me time for a good hot shower, or depending on how late she might be, a good cold one.

At 4 P.M., there was still no sign of OH and no call.

Strange. If OH says she's going to be at a certain place at a certain time, you can count on her being there. And there was no message. I tried to get interested in the reports I needed to read for Saturday's meeting.

Five P.M. came and went and I was beginning to get worried. It wasn't like her not to let me know if she were delayed. I called Daughter Number Three at her office. Yes, they had had lunch together, but her mother had left to go shopping, although she didn't seem to be feeling very well. Now I was really worried.

At 6 P.M. I was about ready to dial 911. I knew she would have called if she could, so the fact that she was this late with no message meant something was very wrong. I decided to start calling the hospitals to see if anyone had been admitted unconscious or in a trance or drunk. The last was rather unlikely since OH rarely touches even wine.

Suddenly the telephone rang. It had to be OH. Thank God! But the voice on the other end was decidedly male.

"Mr. Ed Smith?"

A bit of a shiver slithered up my spine. I said that I was.

"Is your wife's name Marion?"

The shiver transformed itself into an iceberg and lodged itself in the pit of my stomach.

I said that it was.

"OK, I have some news for you."

I could not have been colder had I been sitting stark naked on the Greenland ice cap in a January blizzard.

"Your wife is here."

My wife is here? Here? As in *here*? Right now? My God, what a relief! Tell her to come on down.

"No, you don't understand. She's down there."

I did not expect she'd be at the Albatross in Gander if you say she's here. Here to me means here, right here in MFH. What does this "there" mean?

"What I mean, Mr. Smith, is that your wife is in Room 244, across the hall from you."

Now that gave a whole new meaning to "here." I banged up the phone, ran across the hall and knocked loudly on the door. Who should open it but herself and looking none too happy.

She had come to the hotel less than a half hour behind me, and was told that I hadn't yet turned up and there was no message.

Okay, she thought, that means he's a bit late, but not much, otherwise he'd let me know. By 6 P.M. when I hadn't turned up, she was convinced that I had had an accident and was lying dead or badly maimed in some ditch, saying her name with my last breath.

Little did she know that I was across the hall, freshly showered and waiting for her. And little did I know, of course, that she was across the hall waiting for me. We spent roughly three hours across the hall from each other wondering where the hell the other had gotten to.

By that time, of course, I had a dinner to attend and she had places to go. When we finally found ourselves back at the hotel together it was the wee small hours of the morning and you know how being tired and sleepy affects people our age.

Not a particle.

## The Nuptials

You know me as an expert in parenthood.

Over the years, more by necessity than choice, I have specialized in fatherhood. Last weekend was my graduation in that subject area, magna cum laude. Daughter Number Two was married.

It's all over for me now. My little girl has found another man. The infant I held in my arms and cuddled and changed, who ran to me when she was hurt or when she was happy, who told me her troubles as easily as she told me her dreams, is a married woman. She has someone else. She doesn't need me anymore. I know that. Her mother knows that.

But someone forgot to tell her.

Her grandfather married her. That was touching, especially when he pointed out that twenty-five years ago he had held her in his arms and baptized her. But he reduced us all to absolute jelly when he interrupted the ceremony to sing "I Love You Truly" especially to her. Then she climbed halfway up over the altar rail, wedding dress and all, to give him a hug. Our Kath was never one for conventions.

The morning after her wedding several extended family members were gathered at our house for breakfast preparatory to going their separate ways. Guess who turned up looking for something to eat. Music may be the food of love, but love is no substitute for food. They were hungry, they said. Fair enough. They ate and then left again for their own apartment a few streets over.

But I couldn't help thinking of how things have changed since OH and I were married. We didn't want to see anyone on our honeymoon. OH was so intent on our being alone that she even brought along a crib board to help pass the time. The first three days of our marriage we never even opened the deck of cards. It took another three days to get to the end of one game. Finally we threw the cards and the board out the window. Why? No point in my telling you that. OH will never let it be printed. She and the editors are in cahoots.

Later that same night shortly before supper, I get this call.

"Daddy," a familiar voice said falteringly, "do you have any food in the house? We forgot to get some."

Understandable, I suppose. So guess who we had for supper. Correct. Both of them.

Just in case they had also forgotten a bed, I explained to OH that no way was either or both of them crawling in with us that night. Or any other night.

Even as I write down here in my basement hideaway, a door slams and a voice comes floating down the stairs. "Mommmmmm! Any of my wedding cake left?"

They are like the Biblical poor.

We shall have them with us always.

## Getting Older

It's finally happened.

As my great-uncle William's wife, twenty-five years younger than he, said shortly after their wedding, "I feel old age creeping up on me."

I know the problem is age because Other Half said so.

"Are young people these days getting just a bit louder?" I remarked to her one afternoon over the holidays. Ten of that ilk between the ages of fifteen and twenty-five were congregated in our kitchen. "Or am I getting old?"

She pondered only briefly.

"You're getting old," she said.

"I can't hear you over the racket," I shouted.

"I said," she shouted back, "that you're getting old—and deaf."

"Age does have its blessings," I said, but I don't think anyone heard me.

The crowd on that day was attracted by the idea that after a cold afternoon of snowmobiling our house would be the hot chocolate oasis of the universe. Looking them over from a safe vantage point—the sink where the cups had to be washed—I was struck by the fact that over sixty-six per cent of that lot were actually sleeping at our house on a holiday-permanent basis.

Thinking it over further, I realized that the sleeping part didn't bother me nearly so much as the eating part.

Other Half invited me to run down to the store yesterday afternoon to get four two-litre containers of milk.

"Didn't we get four two-litre containers of milk last night?"

I remember well having to go out into the bleak midwinter while the wolves stayed inside the door. Other Half is unmoved.

"Would you rather they went on the beer?"

"No, but I think it would be easier, not to mention cheaper, if we simply rented somebody's milk cow and tied her up to the verandah. We could run four rubber tubes from each of her watchamacallits to the table and ..."

"You are getting old."

It's a statement I hear more and more and at the oddest hours.

I was somewhat mollified and gratified to find most of the crew in bed when we returned home one night from a friend's house in the admittedly wee small hours. Other Half and I went straight to bed to enjoy the sleep of the just. So many bodies are lying around in the strangest of places that enjoying anything of the unjust is out of the question. You never know when someone is going to pop out from under your bed with an apologetic "Excuse me, Sir; I gotta go to the bathroom."

Anyway, life among the late-hours set was surprisingly quiet that night and we settled down for a long winter's nap. At three-thirty the phone went off by my head, causing me to leap up in the bed and collide with Other Half who was on her way back down. Her reflexes, developed in the days when we were dating, have always been faster than mine.

Do I have to draw you a picture of what a phone call at three-thirty in the morning does to one's heart? The girls were all at home so it couldn't be one of them calling with the devastating news that a hairdo had gone frizzy. Even Number One Son was sleeping somewhere in the house.

When I finally got the thing off the hook and mumbled something approximating "Hello," it turned out to be the parent of one of our "guests." She was calling from a part of the nation where they hadn't had the supper dishes washed yet.

I would say roughly at least three more "stun-Newfie" jokes (which I hate with a passion, including the term "Newfie") came out of that one call alone. I am not at my best in those circumstances. The good news is that I got back to sleep, assuming I had awakened in the first place, in short order.

The bad news is that the damn thing rang again at four-thirty. This time an anxious local mother was looking for a missing daughter who had spent the later part of the evening and earlier part of the morning at our house. I started to check out my room but remembered in time that I am getting old.

Having spent much of my life as an anxious father, I have great sympathy for anxious mothers. We spent the next half-hour or so rousing our offspring and asking for clues to the missing one's whereabouts. Turned out she was simply chatting it up at a girlfriend's house. You know how time flies when you're having fun.

Time does not fly when you're trying to get back to sleep and daylight is pouring in through the frost on your window. Time does not fly when you're trying to get through the day with both eyes screaming to go on strike and numbness spreading from your frontal lobes to your backside. The frontal lobes are your brain, Ma'am, get your mind out of the gutter. The point is that going without sleep, to mention just one of the Big Three, does not tend to make me a happy camper.

Truth is, we enjoy having the young crowd around the house. It's just unfortunate that they have to sleep and eat here as well. Neither our water heater nor our refrigerator was built for the numbers involved.

"Do you find that things tend to get on your nerves more than they used to?" I asked Other Half Monday, "or am I getting old?"

"You're getting ..."

"The question," I said coldly, "was purely rhetorical."

## The Dark Side

"I can't believe you would write something like that!"

That's the abridged version. The whole text is more like the following (sentence structure mine, the words from my dear readers):

"I can't believe that someone raised in a good Christian home by Christian parents with Christian values; someone in the position you're in with a responsibility to uphold Christian virtues and high moral standards; someone with children to look up to you; someone with an education and supposed to be intelligent;

someone who makes the money you make—would even think such thoughts, let alone write them down for all the world to see. Must you expose to the reading public the most irreverent and indecent carnal thoughts that come to your sick mind? Your poor wife must be so ashamed! And I can't bear to think of your dear mother!"

I tell you truly, many's the time I've been moved to tears by such homilies. Many's the time I've vowed to reform so that I no longer give offence to the innocent and the virtuous. No writer worth his salt—whether fishery, road, table or rock—wants his readers to think less of him—or her—whatever.

Despite our protestations to the contrary, only those divinely inspired writers who have something of vast importance to say to the world can afford to disregard the reactions of those lesser beings who exist only to read their greater thoughts. Those of us who do it for the money want to keep our readers happy so that we can continue doing it for the money. With that in mind, I have a confession to make.

It isn't me.

It isn't me who writes this tripe. Oh, it's the same fingers and the same eyes and even the same name, but it isn't me. It isn't the same person at all.

My computer is like a telephone booth. No sooner is it switched on than my persona undergoes drastic change. The conservative, mild-mannered, discreet and restrained personality known to all who love him as Ed Smith is usurped by a flamboyant, devil-may-care, reckless and mischievous rogue who says what he likes and couldn't care less what anyone thinks. He, too, goes by the name of Ed Smith.

I, of course, must take the crap for writing the crap, if you know what I mean. It's the best of all arguments, as Mark Twain knew, for adopting a *nom de plume* which is French for, "No, Ma'am, I didn't write that."

I'm deadly serious about this, in case you're wondering. Literature is full of similar situations: the good Dr. Jekyll and his darker half, the evil Mr. Hyde, and the twin brothers in Steinbeck's *East of Eden.*

Stephen King explored the same theme in his novel *The Dark Half* in which the character created in the mind of a writer assumes a physical identity and speedily dispatches in most unpleasant fashion people he doesn't like. This includes St. John's native and actor what's-his-face Joy, who plays a mean little villain in the movie of the same name and gets what's coming to him.

That's the way it is with us geniuses. Buried deep within is an alter ego trying desperately to get out. Sometimes that "other person" is the darker half that we can usually keep tightly under wraps. Sometimes it's the person we would like to be if only we had the nerve. It's the latter that applies most to writers. Not only can we create the characters we would like to be, but also in the act of writing we can actually become those characters in a relatively safe context.

Exactly the same thing applies to drunks. When alcohol removes the inhibitions, drunks become the persons they really are inside which is sometimes fun and sometimes isn't. Drunks and writers, therefore, have a lot in common, which explains why so many great writers are drunks and so many great drunks are writers. You follow?

Writing removes the inhibitions from a normally sane individual such as myself and lets that other Ed Smith out. Sometimes he will write things in this column that the everyday Ed Smith would never dream of saying.

At times I've been forced to confront this other person and lay down the law.

"Now look here, friend, you're living under my roof and eating my grub and sleeping with my wife, all of which I accept as part of the sacrifice of being a writer. But I simply will not allow you to say those nasty things about TV evangelists or talk about sex as if it were supposed to be fun."

The result is that you never get to see the worst that this other fellow is capable of. He even ends sentences with prepositions.

As far as my "poor wife" is concerned, I get the strong impression that she often prefers the other Ed Smith to me.

My dear mother? I know some very sober and sincere people who wouldn't dream of sitting next to her in church because laughing out loud during prayers is not looked on with favour from the pulpit, especially when my father is in it. My strong suspicion is that this other personality to which I refer got much more nurturing during the formative years than I did.

One final thought. You remember that comment from the more discriminating of my readers about revealing my most irreverent and carnal thoughts? The truth is, I never have.

Not yet.

## From Verse to Worse

A gentleman stopped me in the Zellers Mall off Torbay Road the other day.

I assume he was a gentleman. He looked and dressed like a man of taste and he said he liked my columns, which proved it.

"But," he said, "I wish you'd write more poems in your own inimitable style."

I said I would, especially for him. But since I didn't have time to do anything original this week, what follows are some take-offs on a few of our more famous poems and poets. I hope they'll forgive me. We begin with a Willie Shakespeare sonnet.

*Shall I compare thee to a summer's day?*
*A summer's day in dear old Newfoundland?*
*You are as warm as North winds off the bay.*
*A piece of kelp no colder than your hand.*
*Your love's the fog that settles cold and damp;*
*Your heart's the bellycatter on the beach.*
*The foghorn sounding with its flashing lamp*
*Is many times more lovely than your speech.*
*But you are different in one way, my pet;*
*In Newfoundland, a summer day is wet.*

Okay. So much for that. You may have noticed I shortened the normal sonnet length by approximately four lines, but you had the main idea by then. Shall we take a shot at Robbie Burns?

*"Drink to me only with thine eyes"*
*Is just a lot of bunk.*
*Unless we hit the liquor, dear,*
*I'll never get you drunk.*

I'm sorry. That was not nice. Let's turn to a love sonnet.

*How do I love thee? Let me count the lays*
*And tell you from addition's point of view.*

*As long as we don't skip too many days*
*Or nights, I'll keep on loving you.*
*If "how" is what you're interested in*
*We'll say no more, my missionary friend.*

That one is probably two lines too long already.

Perhaps another poetic form is in order. One of my favourite ballads is Barbry Ellen. Remember it from school?

*'Twas in the merry month of May*
*And June buds they were swellin'*
*Sweet William on his deathbed lay*
*And so did Barbry Ellen.*
*She tried to rouse him to her breast*
*Saying, "We could be complete, Dear."*
*But William said, "I don't like girls;*
*That's why they call me 'sweet,' Dear."*

That's not the way the old story goes, but you have to admit mine is more modern. Shall we try again? With apologies to Alfred, Lord Tennyson.

*Break, break, break,*
*On thy cold grey stones, O Sea.*
*And I would I could see the codfish*
*That once used to swim in thee.*

*O well for the union leaders,*
*Whose rhetoric comes from their lungs.*
*O well for the politicians,*
*Whose guts are all in their tongues.*

*But the boats we used to sail in*
*Are hauled up on the shore.*
*And the good soft feel of a slimy cod*
*Is a thing I shall see no more.*

Wouldn't that break your heart? We're on a roll here, people. Let us carry on. Remember this one by Lord Byron?

*She walks in beauty, like the night*
*Of cloudless climes and starry skies*
*But if you saw her in the light*
*'Twould make you gasp and stretch your eyes.*

Not good enough? You'll feel better about this next one. The first line is from Stevenson's *Christmas at Sea*. The "sheets," as every sailor knows, are the ropes used to raise and lower the sails. Why am I telling you all this?

*The sheets were frozen hard, and they cut the naked hand;*
*The long johns were like ice in which no legs would ever stand;*
*The blouses and the panties might as well have been in Nain;*
*And the whole clothesline was swinging under tons of freezing rain.*

You'll have to forgive me, folks.
I've had a hard week.

# Out of Eden

Benny Hill is dead. So is Frankie Howard.

Both gone. Gone, like yesterday's innocence, like yesterday's dreams, like the blush on a young bride's cheeks. Two of the greatest comic geniuses of our time, gone. I don't feel that well myself.

Perhaps you never knew them by name, but you knew them. Hill and Howard were the naughty boys of British comedy, the masters of the nudge-nudge, wink-wink, sexist, slapstick style of laughter that included the likes of Hattie Jakes and Sydney James of "Carry on ..." fame.

Hill was best known for his series *The Benny Hill Show* which the BBC finally axed as blatant sexual innuendo, but which places like France and Japan found hilarious and irresistible. Howard was popular on this side of the Pond with his series *Up Pompeii.* We used to gather at each other's houses for the weekly late-night viewing of *Up Pompeii,* and ooohed and aaahed over the double entendres and characters with names like Nauseous and Letittica.

At times they were vulgar, often they were irreverent, and always they were earthy. And as young adults we loved them. Remember Frankie Howard's long meaningful "oooooohhh" with the rising inflection and the "oh-dear-me" expression?

The women in these comedies were always round and buxom, and the men lecherous, leering types who spent their time looking up skirts and down blouses and making appropriate remarks all the while.

It was another world. A world that was earthy and sexist and politically incorrect. A world of knickers and burlesque and bottom-pinching. It was a world where "gay" meant happy and a long, low whistle was a compliment instead of an insult. Where men and women laughed at the same things and the sexes were not at war. It was another world.

It was another age. An age where we could laugh at foolishness, something we don't do well today. Foolishness was simply that, with no hidden agendas and no political targets. It was an age where we could laugh at sex, again a lost art. Sex, like foolishness, wasn't a matter for societal comment. It was an individual matter of boy chasing girl and vice versa with all the attendant antics.

Today sex, like foolishness, has gone serious, and laughing at either is bound to offend someone.

Hill and Howard laughed at sex. They found comedy in our enslavement to it, admitted or otherwise, and joyed in making us look ridiculous as we pursued it.

There are many today who condemn the comedy of Benny Hill and Frankie Howard as sexist and titillating, vulgar and cheap, coarse and offensive. And without doubt, their routines had elements of all of these.

Yet, I don't recall ever hearing the kind of language on *Up Pompeii* that you get in practically any modern film, or even on CBC's *Here and Now*. Hill and Howard were bible-toting pastors compared with Eddie Murphy or Bette Midler or the news. In the world of Frankie and Benny, vulgarity and coarseness were in the eye of the beholder. In today's comedies, it's forced down your throat. And by the time you get past the social or gender comment the humour is long gone.

The likes of Hill and Howard were vulgar without being profane, and irreverent without being sacrilegious. It ain't so anymore.

Perhaps it is only in looking back that we hear the innocence in the laughter and see the candour in the mirth. Nothing is innocent in the nineties. We have eaten from the apple and our nakedness convinces us of our vices. It is too serious a matter to laugh about.

Benny Hill was not a vulgar person. He didn't go on *Oprah* and talk about his family as if they belonged in a zoo, or his life as though it were a psychiatrist's nightmare. Although no recluse, he was a private man who lived with his mother until her death a few years ago and rarely gave interviews. And a couple of weeks ago he died alone.

Only a few days separated the deaths of Hill and Howard, almost as if together they wanted to escape from a world which no longer had any room for them.

Charlie Chaplin once said that Hill was a true comic genius and one of the few people alive who could make him laugh.

In retrospect, the worse that can be said for Benny Hill and Frankie Howard is that they reflected the values of a male-dominated world where women were exploited at every turn.

The best we can say is that they made millions laugh the good, old-fashioned belly laugh that cleanses and recreates and heals. Someday I would like for someone to say as much for me.

Hill and Howard have stopped making us laugh forever. But they still have a timeless message we would do well to heed. Lighten up, world. Take a Valium. Learn to laugh.

Benny Hill and Frankie Howard are dead and we will never see their like again.

Long live the clown princes.

# The Season of the Worm

Food for worms.

That's what Shakespeare said we ultimately become. It was not one of his more inspiring word pictures. It wasn't one of his most poetic lines. I'd just as soon he hadn't said it at all. But he did. He was probably talking about worms in the generic sense as including everything that creeps and crawls within the soil that finally covers us. Lovely.

But today I'm talking real worms. The kind you dig in the garden with your prong and reeve onto your hook by the side of the pond. This is the time of year when worms have their raison d'être, which is French for "excuse for being alive." The essence of a worm's existence is validated in a hook and a line and a bamboo pole. This is the season of the worm.

When you get right down to it, worms lead a dog's life. I've worked for years to get worms established in my garden because they're good for the soil. Nature's little engineers is what they are, letting the air in through their little tunnels and enriching the soil with their little bowel movements.

But you know what happens to the first worm I see when I dig up the garden in the spring? Right into the old worm bucket. Doesn't matter if you're planning to go fishing tomorrow or in September. The destiny of all worms is to be strung on a hook and drowned kicking and screaming in a large body of water.

Frankly, I don't know if worms scream or not. Perhaps they do in their own way, but happily I have not found out what way that is. It's bad enough to see them kicking.

Actually, the worms that come to their end on the point of a hook are the lucky ones. Many's the worm that has met a more gruesome death in the pocket of my old fishing jacket, cooped up in some small bottle and left to rot. My strong advice to anyone who lets that happen is not to remove the cover from the bottle. The stench of rotten worms is responsible for at least fifty per cent of atmospheric ozone loss. Doesn't do much for your jacket, either.

The opposite tragedy to that is putting a plastic bucket full of worms in your greenhouse and forgetting all about them for the rest of the summer. They dry to a snarbuckle. Not only is this bad for the worm, but stringing a dried worm on your hook is not one of life's simpler tasks. The good thing about it is that being already deceased, the worm doesn't feel a thing.

It's a moot point, of course, as to whether worms feel anything while being reeved unto a hook when they're alive. Only a few people have given the matter much thought or cared much one way or the other. I'm not one of them.

I don't suppose being plucked from the soil by a ravenous bird is any fun, either, but that's yet another indignity that your poor worm is forced to endure. Beats being a taxpayer, of course, where you're plucked by the government on a continuous basis. Being plucked is not what it's cracked up to be in either case.

There are several kinds of worms, classified from a fishing point of view. The first is your small red affair found in manure heaps and known by the appropriate name of manure worm. Actually, "manure" worm isn't what it's called, but it means the same thing. I can't say the other word in a family newspaper. Let's just call them S-worms, as in K-cars or J-cloths.

S-worms are useless for serious fishing. It takes seven or eight to make a decent size bait and three casts later there's nothing left on your hook. They simply fall apart in the water. This is extremely frustrating for the fisherperson who has a tendency to utter a short, four-letter word each time it happens. Which is undoubtedly why they're called S-worms.

The second type of worm is what's normally found in typical garden soil. Two or three inches long, sort of pale from lack of exposure to the sun and much tougher than S-worms. These fit beautifully onto a bamboo-size fishing hook and are hard enough to stay on for several casts and perhaps two or three trout, if they're biting good. We call those just plain worms, or if you like P-worms. P-worms are the fishing favourites.

The third type of worm found in gardens throughout the land is the E-worm. The E stands for "eumongous." These things are eight or ten inches long and about two inches wide. You find them crawling around your lawn at night when they come out to eat grass, lumps of dirt and mice. They're difficult to put on any hook smaller than a cod jigger. If you attach only one end of these things to the hook and let the rest of it swim free, they have a tendency to attack pan-size trout and frighten them off.

The only workable method for fishing with E-worms is mutilation. You cut them in usable lengths with an axe, not unlike the procedure for beheading hens. You need a strong stomach for this exercise and something to wipe the place up with afterward.

E-worms are used for dissecting in biology labs when they run out of cats.

Yes, consider the lowly worm. It gets walked on, run over, mutilated, drowned, dried up and eaten. Still, with infinite patience it goes on enriching the soil, feeding the birds, catching our trout and otherwise making our lives so much the better just by being here.

Does the worm feel resentful or bitter? Again, I don't know. But if it does, it ultimately has its revenge. Shakespeare was right, of course.

All it has to do is wait.

# Family Ties

Daughter Number Two (DN2) and Son-In-Law (SIL) have just become homeowners.

Their house is on the street behind ours and one lot over. Thus they are separated from us by the width of our neighbour's garden. OH and I have speculated about what it means to have DN2 and her family living within half a stone's throw of the family hearth. We have speculated at some length.

DN2 and SIL dropped by today to talk about the wonders of owning your own home. The main thing, they said, was this marvellous sense of independence, of having to rely on nothing and no one, of being your own person and doing your own thing.

SIL's enthusiasm was dampened only a little when he discovered that my old pickup is in the shop for the next week or so having the gas tank replaced. He needs the truck, he pointed out, not only to help them move from their apartment next weekend, but also to get manure for DN2's new flower garden.

DN2 took it in stride. While they were waiting for the truck to be repaired, she suggested to SIL he could begin digging up the area in their new garden where she intended to plant vegetables.

SIL agreed that this was a good idea and did I have a spade he could use, and a rake. General enthusiasm shot up again, especially when DN2 discovered that she could get some leftover seeds from her mother.

Actually, our daughter, far-seeing soul that she is, has been growing things in little peat pots for several weeks preparatory to planting same in her own independent little garden. DN2 never does things by half. She has dozens of various size pots containing all manners of plants, all of which are currently residing in my greenhouse.

The twenty or so tomato plants, fourteen cucumbers and sundry assorted vegetables which I laboriously planted in the greenhouse are nowhere to be seen. They are hidden under dozens of various size peat pots containing everything from pot to peppers (not really, it just sounds cute), all belonging to the independent and proud DN2 and SIL.

It has occurred to me that on a quiet night when the windows are open one can easily hear a baby cry from their house to here. My initial reaction was so what? This is their baby and therefore their problem. Grandparents are not for when babies cry. Grandparents are for when babies coo and laugh and do cute things. They do anything other than cute things and they are immediately whisked back to their parents.

On reflection, however, the implications of being able to hear the screams of your daughter's colicky infant are potentially horrendous. Will OH just lie there and bask in the satisfaction that this thing ain't ours? Not a chance. Will she slip silently out of bed, without waking me, and rush across to her daughter's side to give aid and comfort in the dead of night? Not a chance. OH will turn to me for aid and comfort in the dead of night, as she so often does.

"Ed, are you awake? Do you hear that? That's little Edwina crying her poor little heart out. Ed, wake up! Do you think she's sick? Do you think they hear her? Poor DN2 must be out of her mind. Perhaps we should call the doctor for them. Do you think I should go over? There's something definitely wrong with that child! Perhaps we should bring her over here and give them a break. Come on, Ed, let's go get her!"

I have nightmares over that last bit. But facts are facts. Fact, DN2 and SIL are having a baby. Fact, babies cry. Fact, if this one is anything like its mother was we're in for a rough time.

I can see it now. SIL, who's a carpenter, will make a little basket for our First Grandchild (FG) which will fit on the clothesline connecting his yard with the neighbour's which is connected with our yard in the same way. Our clothesline comes right into our back porch through shutters constructed for the purpose so that OH can put out her clothes without going out into the freezing cold. Talk about being pampered.

DN2 and SIL will simply put their baby into the basket when they're tired of it and shoot it off through space in our general direction. With only a brief stopover at the neighbour's place to change clotheslines, she'll be in our back porch crying for her grandfather. I have nightmares about that, too.

I don't know how the neighbours feel about it. Perhaps they can be bribed not to allow any travelling through their airspace. Perhaps I can nail up the shutters. Perhaps we can move.

Now you're thinking that my reaction to my daughter and her family living so close to us is entirely negative. Nothing could be further from the truth. There are thousands of reasons I'm over-joyed to have DN2, SIL and FG right next door. Thousands. OH and I were up half the night just a little while ago thinking about it. Thousands.

Okay, what with Number One Son away to college most of the year, I suppose SIL could give me some help with the six or eight cords of wood I burn every winter, every spring and most of every summer. And shovelling tons of snow from the driveway is not recommended for a man of my age, but with a strapping SIL across the way ... And when I haul up my boat in October ... And when I need someone to go up on the roof and clean the chimney ... And when the car won't start on cold winter mornings ... Yes indeed! Thousands of reasons! Thousands.

I can say it without reservation or hesitation.

What a joy it is for a man to have his family around him!

## What Child is This?

I am a grandfather!

The other day I received a letter from a lady who was none too happy with one of my columns. The reason she was upset with only one, it seems, was that one was all she'd read and she didn't show any great interest in perusing any others. She said, among other things, that an "intelligent, young" person such as myself should have better sense, or words to that effect.

That letter came just in time, I can tell you. I forgot everything she said that wasn't what you'd call complimentary and focused on that word "young." If ever there is a time to be called "young" by someone of the opposite sex, it is the same week in which you become a grandfather. Thank you, Ma'am, and God bless you and your seed forever!

Daughter Number Two presented the world with Samantha Rae yesterday. I knew all along she'd be a girl and said so with conviction. Science and folklore experts did their thing and proclaimed it to be a boy. So did Son-In-Law, who had the audacity to place a small wager on the matter, which I, of course, accepted and I, of course, won.

How did I know it was a girl? Simple. On the night Daughter and hubby told us she was with child, I dreamed a dream. I was driving my boat up the bay towards home, and sitting on my lap with her little hands grasping the steering wheel was a little girl.

Dreams worked for people in the Bible all the time. Just because I'm not in the Bible is no reason it couldn't work for me. It's not my fault I'm not there.

Daughter called with the news while I was having a private meeting with the Minister of Health. He probably won't mind my telling you that not only did the lovely lady who's his secretary put the call through, but the Minister left his office so that I could talk to my daughter in private. Touch of class there, Sir, and thank you!

Grandparents. It's a whole new feeling. You know all the tired old jokes about having to sleep with a grandmother from now on (as though there were a law about it), and how you're supposed to feel really old and over the hill and all that stuff. Forget it.

As I said to OH just last night, "Grandma, what big eyes you have!" And she turned to me with that look in her eyes and those three little words: "Ed, shut up!"

This feeling is special and different, as our friends who are grandparents told us it would be, but it took me awhile to figure out why. It has nothing to do with having all the fun of a child without any of the work and responsibility, although I sincerely hope that principle applies. Or with being able to propel her back over the clothesline to Daughter's house when she loads her diapers or puts a rock through the neighbour's window. Or seeing in another new generation the reassurance of immortality and BS like that. None of it explains why a grandchild is so special. But I'll tell you what does.

It's simply that this is your child having a child. The connection is what makes it extraordinary. The mother in that bed yesterday was our baby, and for a moment I saw her again through the years and the nursery glass with her little clenched fists and her small heart face. It, too, was only yesterday.

Then suddenly here she is with another small miracle lying beside her with the same little clenched fists and the same little heart-shaped face. Actually, she looks more like Daughter Number Three, but I'm trying to wax poetic here. And she's a perfect little human being, except that she has her father's ears.

The big question now, of course, is what will this grandchild call me? OH doesn't seem to care if the kid calls her Mammy Yokum, but it matters to me. I'm not sure why but it does.

In my view, there should be a law against "Grandpaw" and "Granddad," and the penalty for breaking it should involve the removal of body parts. "Grandfather" is a generic title and should only be used when there are at least three "greats" in front of it. "Poppy" is a flower that grows in France and "Pops" is a symphony orchestra in Boston.

Understand, please, that these are my own views entirely and in no way represent the feelings of the Central Newfoundland Regional College, the Newfoundland Hospital and Nursing Home Association or any other group with which I have any association. At least, not as far as I know or they're willing to admit.

My son-in-law, the new father, in an effort to get back at me for having to pay off the bet, insists that he's going to train the child to call me "Poppy Ed." That will be the second biggest mistake of his young life.

In answer to your unspoken question, I would prefer my granddaughter called me "Ed." That's my name. It was good enough for my parents. It's good enough for my friends. It should be good enough for my grandchildren. Samantha and Edward. Sam and Ed. Has a certain ring to it, don't you think? Sam and Ed are off fishing. Ed and Sam are gone for a walk.

"What'd you do in school today, Sam?"

"Nothing, Ed boy."

Sounds good to me. Unfortunately, I seem to be a minority of one.

The truth is, it's not bad being a grandfather, not bad at all.

As my father said, putting it all in perspective, "If you get to feeling sorry for yourself, remember that I'm a great-grandfather." And as my mother said with even greater perspective, "I can't wait to be a great-great-grandmother!"

With a little luck she will, and with a little luck I'll get to have this marvellous feeling again and again.

It is only the beginning.

## The Prodigal Dog

Perhaps some of you will remember Tiki.

Tiki is our Heinz 57 mutt, due to celebrate his eighteenth birthday in a couple of months. Eighteen is one hundred and twenty-six in human years, which is old in anyone's language. Eighteen years with Tiki is enough to earn anyone an extra shine on the halo and an extra star or two in the crown.

I, who love dogs, have in confrontations with him lost my patience, my dignity and my religion, none of which have been seen since. But difficult as I have found the intervening years between this weekend and the day Tiki first arrived, I have to admit there is one who has suffered and endured more. Tiki was put on this earth by an unkind deity specifically to irritate OH.

Tom's dog—the one that put his backside in the water to get a drink—looks like a Harvard Ph.D. alongside Tiki. He has what I call behavioural dyslexia, which means he does everything bassackwards. Call him to come and he'll take off. Tell him to get lost and he'll come running. Tell him to sit up and he'll roll over. Demand that he use the great outdoors to heed the call of nature and he'll ignore you. And he has one other extremely maddening quality. Tiki is capable of laughing at you. I know, because most of the time he's laughing at me.

Tiki and OH have a love-hate relationship. Perhaps that's not entirely accurate. I have never once seen any indication of love from either of them toward the other. Hate may be too strong a word, too, because OH feeds and waters the poor brute regularly, and he in turn tries hard not to show how he feels about her.

But it is mutual tolerance at best. To be fair to OH, it's hard to be enamoured of something that pees on your furniture, throws up on your carpet and treats you like dirt. To be fair to Tiki, he is a dog. A slob even for a dog, but still a dog.

At eighteen, Tiki has reached the bottom of his behavioural cycle. Although he seems happy enough with life as he finds it, the years have not been kind to him. He is stone-cold deaf, which doesn't matter a lot because he never comes when you call him anyway, and partially blind. His belly has never risen more than a couple of inches above the floor, but now a shag carpet is enough to drag him to a complete halt. He has long since lost the use of reverse gear, or more likely forgotten he had it.

It's all he can do to navigate the hallway, shivering and wobbling with each step, until at last he reaches his destination under his favourite chair and flops exhausted.

And Tiki is incontinent. Actually, he never has been completely continent in his whole life, but we put that down to a personality rather than a physiological problem.

Then last Friday Tiki turned up missing.

OH put him out for his daily constitutional in the dog-run around supper time, knowing he would bark as usual when he wanted to come in, which is normally just before he goes to the toilet on the porch floor. When he had gone an inordinately long time without barking someone went to check on him and there he was, gone. A hue and cry was raised and the search was on, with OH more or less joining in.

It had snowed hard all that day and at night the temperature plummeted to its normal minus eighteen or twenty. Number One Son, OH and I searched until three in the morning before concluding it was hopeless. For months we'd been expecting to find him dead in the basement or under his chair. Since he couldn't walk more than a few feet without falling, we assumed he had probably had a heart attack and dropped in the snow. It wouldn't take long to bury him completely.

At least that's what we hoped. The thought of him digging his way out of the run and into a drift that he couldn't get out of, there to perish, was something even OH found hard to contemplate. But shovel and stomp as we might, no sign of the mongrel was to be found.

We decided to put an ad on the local TV channel, just in case, but we all knew it was hopeless. Tiki had inspired his last case of bad language.

I cleaned up the basement floor with a mixture of Javex, Lysol and hydrochloric acid and washed out the dog bedding, remarking that at least the basement wouldn't stink anymore. OH vacuumed the living room, saying that at least she wouldn't have to do it twice a day anymore. I suggested we could now start thinking about the new carpeting we had needed for so long and refused to get while Tiki was still doing his thing.

This afternoon, the third day since the Disappearance, Daughter Number Two and Son-In-Law Number One came to visit. Daughter had our granddaughter in her arms, and Son-in-law had Tiki, tail wagging feebly, in his. Seems they had gone for a snowmobile ride out on the bay, and couldn't believe their eyes when they ran upon this little, brown, furry thing wobbling along on unsteady legs and heading in the general direction of the British Isles.

We don't know how he got that far, how he survived the nights of intense cold or why he was running away from home to begin with. There were tears in OH's eyes and a little later I saw her with her head in her hands muttering, "Why me? Why me?" She confided to me that she had no intention of getting saved, not altogether a surprise for her fundamentalist friends, because if Tiki ever found out she was going to heaven he'd be there to torment her.

"Then it won't be heaven," I said.

"Exactly," she replied in a lifeless voice.

But later in the evening when she thought no one was looking, I saw OH with a Kraft Cheese Slice in her hand looking for the dog.

"Here, Lazarus," she was calling quietly, "welcome home."

## All in the Family

A Toronto chap was describing his first hunting experience in Newfoundland.

"There we were," he declared dramatically, "deep in the Newfundlund wilderness with the black spruce so thick we had to turn sideways to get through it. Suddenly from out of nowhere this thousand-pound bull moose with antlers at least six feet wide came running through the trees straight at us!"

"Just a minute, Bill," broke in one of his listeners. "If the trees were so thick you couldn't walk through them, how could a moose with antlers six feet wide run through them?"

"Why," said Bill after only a moment's pause, "he had to pull in his horns the way we do sometimes."

And that's precisely what I have to do this week—pull in my horns, eat crow, chew on humble pie and all the rest of it.

Long-time and faithful readers of this claptrap, and surely Lord there must be one (you still read this, don't you Mom?), will remember a column not too long ago in which I lamented the fact that not one Upper Canadian had thought to send me so much as a card for our fortieth birthday as a province.

I have to admit to feeling kind of bitter at the time. No one up there cares about us, I complained. They didn't want us forty years ago and they don't love us now. Pitiful, it was.

Well, my dear! When that stuff hit the *Toronto Star*, which has the sublime good taste to carry "The View" on occasion, the sheep hit the fan, I can tell you. Our cousins in far-off and better-off Ontario were nothing less than chagrined—absolutely and totally chagrined. I've rarely seen so much chagrin piled up in one place.

And what happened? It's hard to believe, but I've been inundated with birthday cards from Upalong. Not a word of a lie! Wellll, after looking it up in my Funk and Wagnall's and reading this over, I find that inundated is perhaps too strong a word. "Dear Abby" is inundated. Erma Bombeck is inundated. For me, "sprinkled" is closer to it. I've been sprinkled with birthday cards.

Now isn't that nice? They really care about us up there!

And something else. Many of the notes read "to Ed Smith and fellow Newfoundlanders." They actually remembered all of us. I thought briefly of getting the cards in question copied and distributed to every Newfoundland household, but discretion and my wife advised strongly against it.

The overriding message on each of these marvellous missives was: "Happy birthday, and we're sorry we missed it!" And again I say, isn't that nice?!

One lovely lady from Cambridge said there were at least seven thousand Newfoundlanders living in her town. I don't know who counted them, but without being rude I can practically guarantee that isn't correct. Chances are the person taking the census didn't bother to ask about the brother-in-law staying with the family until he finds a job of work or the cousin who's up having a baby or the sister who's looking for a husband or the in-laws visiting for the winter. If seven thousand is the official count you can bet your fish and brewis that the real figure is somewhere around twenty-one thousand.

If you don't believe me, run outside early next Sunday morning and start singing the "Ode to Newfoundland" at the top of your lungs. See how many strangers with tears running down their cheeks turn up on your lawn before you get to the second verse.

You don't know the "Ode to Newfoundland"? That's okay. There's lots you don't know about us yet, but now that we're part of the family you'll learn.

A lady from Prince Edward Island told me she would like to have some Newfoundland "squeal." You wouldn't believe the stuff that went through my mind trying to figure out what that was. But finally I got it. She wanted a bottle of that infamous and deadly alcoholic concoction called "Newfoundland Screech."

Perhaps in PEI the stuff produces only a sophisticated squeal, but if that's the case they're watering it down. In Newfoundland little squeals don't satisfy us at all.

Another lady ... I don't understand why it is that the vast majority of people who write to me are women. Thanks be to God they don't publish my picture in the *Star* or I'd really be inundated. On the other hand, I have no problem at all keeping up with the mail from the Great Northern Peninsula where my profile does grace the local press. Strange.

Where were we? Oh yes. Another lady from Paris (Ontario!) wrote a marvellous seven-page epistle describing her adventures while holidaying in the Tenth. What there was to see, she saw. What there was to do, she did. Our Tourism Department should have someone like her on the payroll. But then we'd be swamped with tourists and that would only make my father mad.

Last year, he met three other fishermen (two of them mainlanders) within three days on his favourite salmon river, and he's been grumpy ever since.

"Might as well move to Ontario for the summer," he growled, "and leave the whole darn province to 'em."

But from me on behalf of all of us to all of you—thanks for being so very thoughtful. There's just this one little thing.

I didn't get one present.

## The Unkindest Cut of All

I have obviously been getting much too serious in this column.

Faithful readers will recall my last two topics as dealing with: (a) government's attempts to privatize most of what government is responsible for; and (b) the "doom-and-gloom" prophets who in this province's current economic woes have us down and counted out even before we have begun to fight.

Well, my dear, you talk about your reaction! Phone calls and letters galore. In (b), I have been called by people in high places an ambassador for cheeriness and good times. And in (a), I have been told in no uncertain terms, concerning my frank confusion on the Hydro deal, that ignorance is no excuse for anyone, especially me.

You see the problem? People are starting to take me seriously, for Pete's sake. Next thing you know I'll be winning awards for outstanding journalism and columnism, and people will begin expecting me to say serious things about weighty matters. The problem with that is I'd have to start thinking serious things about weighty matters and I don't have either the time or the inclination.

So it is high time I put an end to this serious business and frolicked in more familiar pastures. In this column, therefore, I wish to discuss the much-neglected topic of appendectomy scars.

I don't know what you and your mate do for kicks. Actually, it's none of my business, although thinking about the possibilities can be fun. Neither are the nocturnal habits of OH and me any of your concern, even when they're not always nocturnal. Point is, none of us have any business in the other's bedroom, unless, of course, we have been given some type of lawful entry.

Nevertheless, and despite OH's anticipated strong objections, I will tell you something we did that caused at least me deep guilt and made a lifelong impression on OH. We did it just the once and just as well, too. It's not something you expect to happen on a regular basis and probably wouldn't be healthy if it did.

On our wedding night we took a break from playing crib and compared appendectomy scars. I guess it's the sort of crazy thing newlyweds do when they're being shy and sensitive. Anyway, to this day the details stand out in my mind as clear as a Clyde Wells talk on constitutional ethics. Mine, you see, turned out to be ever so much larger than hers.

OH has just the tiniest thread of a pale little line about an inch long. It's very feminine and ladylike. My stomach looks as though it were hit by lightning. The scar is several inches long and was obviously made by a chainsaw with a very dull chain. It ain't a pretty sight which is why I generally keep it covered up, especially in winter.

OH was greatly distressed that such unwarranted damage had been done to my innocent person. But after she calmed down we discussed the possible reasons there should be such a difference in our respective incisions.

The first to occur to me was that her doctor was sober, but I was being facetious, sort of. My operation was done in 1948, hers in 1962. Perhaps the respective scars represent the advances made in cutting and suturing over that period. On the other hand, perhaps I had a very large appendix. OH said gently there was nothing about me to suggest that that was the case.

For anaesthetic they stuck something over my face and poured ether into it. I kicked and screamed like a stuck pig, and finally they brought in enough personnel to hold me down until I was put to sleep. This probably explains why I got the ugly stick for a scar. The doctor was in a hurry and I was still kicking when he started cutting. They did that with seals, you know. OH was given a little needle and told to count to ten. She never made it, of course, having been educated in St John's schools.

My operation was done in Newfoundland, OH's in New Brunswick. Are NB doctors better trained in minor surgery? We finally came to the conclusion that my doctor had something else on his mind at the time.

The operation can still be fraught with danger. Not long ago—and this is the gospel truth for me—a chap went in for an appendectomy at a Toronto hospital. He awoke from the anaesthetic with his appendix where it always was (although the article didn't say how he knew that right away), and only empty space where his testicles used to be (the article didn't need to get specific on that one). And don't forget, as men measure time in B.C. and A.D., this was P.B.—pre-Bobbitt.

I know we sometimes have unreasonable expectations of our medical people and expect them to be perfect, like our clergypersons and municipal politicians. But is it too much to ask that they know the difference between the appendix and the testicles, or even their respective positions in the human body?

The hospital was quite apologetic and offered to rectify the error immediately. This, of course, meant having another try at removing the appendix. They said nothing about putting the other things back. The patient was somewhat upset, the article went on, and was suing the hospital for the unlawful removal of parts.

So what does all this have to do with anything? Absolutely nothing, except I wanted to prove something.

I am not a total stranger to frivolity

# And Still Champions!

The *Guinness Book of Records* should be looking at us.

Newfoundlanders, I mean. Newfoundlanders and Labradorians, to be correct. Personally, and with all due respect to the Peoples of the North, "Newfoundland and Labrador" always sounds to me like "Grand Falls/Windsor" and about as necessary. I see with boundless relief that the good people of Clarenville and Shoal Harbour have abandoned the dual-name syndrome. God bless 'em.

But it seems whatever you call us that once again we in this province have excelled in the marital arts. For the umpteenth time in a row, *Maclean's* has voted us the greatest lovers in Canada. It was all over the front page of the magazine last week.

Surely you saw it. Or perhaps, as the article suggested, you were too busy making records. Whatever, there it was in black and white, the naked truth. Despite economic calamity, social upheaval and climatic chaos, Newfoundlanders continue to make love more often than anyone else in Canada.

I tell you the truth, people; I don't know how much longer we can keep it up.

This is nothing new for us, right? We've been winning this award for as long as they've been keeping records. Indeed, we have always been humbly aware of our proficiency in this area, and didn't need anyone from Upalong to tell us so. Nevertheless, it's nice to be recognized for excellence in your chosen field. This survey had some new twists which I found quite fascinating. For the first time *Maclean's* got into actual statistics, and these turned out to be somewhat startling. We in this blessed place, for example, make love an average of ten times a month, including February in non-leap years. That's roughly twelve hundred times a decade, which may leave some of you feeling somewhat deprived. I'm truly sorry.

Ten times a month. On the average. Far be it from me to question those figures, but I wondered about it some. Our poker club tossed the issue around a bit and admitted that they, too, were a mite puzzled by the frequency indicated. This would mean, you see, that there are those who are considerably lower than ten— probably mainlanders who moved here years ago and great-grandparents.

It means, too, that some of us go at it considerably more often than the average, and there was substantial discussion as to who these folks might be. Age seemed to have little to do with it since those surveyed ranged from the twenties to the fifties. But names were mentioned and factors such as political affiliation and religious persuasion weighed and considered. We came to no conclusions that can be reported.

Another interesting issue raised by the survey was the reasons given for this special gift granted solely, it seems, to Newfoundlanders. While most of it was conjecture, the points raised are worthy of consideration. One of these is that, despite the lack of employment, Newfoundlanders still want to work. This also dispels the myth that we will work only for stamps. Or only for ten weeks. If we enjoy what we're doing

Newfoundlanders will work with a will and a half for as long as it takes.

A second reason had to do with entertainment. There's not much entertainment around, said one chap, so we have to make our own. You can see his point. With money so scarce, what else can we afford? Sex is certainly the most fun you can have without cash, unless you have the misfortune to be in downtown St. John's. And it's definitely the most fun you can have without laughing. I'm told that as long as you keep the lights off, most women won't laugh at all, which is comforting.

The third reason given for our propensity for sexual activity was simply that we don't have anything else to do. Personally, I've never found that reason to apply, but perhaps it's an individual thing.

I did hear of a couple in Millertown Junction years ago who lived close to the railway tracks and had seventeen children as a result. The train used to come through every morning at six and wake us, explained the wife, and it was too early to get up and too late to go back to sleep.

The article reported other people as saying that when couples cuddle together for warmth in the cold Newfoundland nights, things tend to happen. Newfoundlanders, in other words, see sex as a viable alternative to being cold. Actually, and according to the article, we see sex as a viable alternative to just about anything, including eating and sleeping.

Statistics will tell you—and this is the truth—that a person's level of education is a prime factor in the quality and quantity of love-making. People with Ph.D.'s will do just about anything any-time, while those who dropped out of Grade Two aren't all that interested usually, and when they are it's just as well that they weren't, if you follow.

Now, if Newfoundland has an illiteracy rate of almost fifty per cent, according to some, how does that explain our sexual vitality? The conclusions reached by one of these sets of stats are obviously wrong. You must decide for yourself which one. The ten-times-a-month bit really puzzled my poker club buddies. We talked about it for hours. This can't be right, we said. In our experience the figures are not reliable or valid and should never be reported for the truth. But finally we hit upon what we thought might be the explanation. Not one of us in our club had been interviewed in the *Maclean's* survey, and so none of us were included in the figures. Aha, we said, that's it.

That explains why the average is so low.

## The Write People

WANL.

Say it through your nose and it sounds like the distressed cry of a constipated duck.

It isn't. WANL is the Writers' Alliance of Newfoundland and Labrador, of which I'm proud to be a member. To ask why I'm a member would be unkind in the extreme, and possibly even ignorant.

I, my dear, am no less than a member-at-large of the WANL executive. Try saying that through your nose.

We've just had our AGM and conference on the West Coast, which from this time forth will probably be known as a centre for cultural excellence, at least in the immediate area of the Deer Lake Motel, Room 156.

To be honest, I wasn't sure I wanted to go. You've heard those stories about writers, especially when they get together. Hard drinking, rowdy parties, uninhibited indulging of all the appetites, everything to excess. The more I thought about it, the more it sounded like a great time.

I did not, of course, repeat these thoughts to Other Half in the fear that she would not let me go, or worse still, want to go with me.

I did consult her on what to wear. The choices were simple: the "starving artist" outfit of torn blue jeans, dirty sneakers and a plaid shirt; or the more "with it" image of baggy pants, shirt open to the navel and blue tam. She suggested a tweed jacket with leather elbows, straight stem pipe (preferably unlit), glasses and a black Labrador on a leash.

Sometimes I wonder if Other Half takes my writing seriously.

Actually, my concerns were not confined to dress. Never before had I approached the charmed circle of those creative souls whose art is written expression. Poets who make music with words and novelists who strip life to the core. Freelancers, playwrights and columnists "who through long hours of darkness/and nights devoid of ease" still hack away. Others.

I was worried sick. What kind of people are writers, anyway? Real writers, I mean. Popular opinion suggested one could expect anything from freaks to parasites. With the possible exception of the "Others" group, I hadn't the least idea of what to expect from anyone. Would I like them? Would they like me? Does it matter a damn? And so on.

But I had to go. I had to go because it was there, like Everest. So I went.

Talk about your shattering of myths. Not one single freak did I encounter, not one. The most off-the-wall person in the place was a waitress who liked to tell jokes. At the hospitality suite, the drug of preference was coffee, and the most abundant liquid, milk. I've seen more beer at missionary meetings. This is not to say there weren't some amongst us who managed to find a smattering of stronger stuff, but next day they stood out like sore heads.

And although I searched and searched, not one solitary orgy could I find. Perhaps I just didn't know where to look, but I'd rather not think that was the case.

When we all sat down at our AGM you could have been at a combined meeting of the Ladies' Aid and Church Men's Club. Some were pregnant, some were knitting and some were reading papers. And the meeting went on for four hours.

From a non-speaking distance, writers seem to be people like everyone else. They walk upright and get mayonnaise on their mouths from the sandwiches. They laugh and get tired and sleep on beds, at least as far as I know.

But writers are not like everyone else. They have this amazing creative energy that never rests. Writers are always writing, even when they're doing something else. If a photographer sees the world through a lens, the writer sees it through a pen. They may be talking to you about the weather, and at the same time a new poem or another play or a different plot twist is taking shape in their minds.

I learned a few other things about them, too.

Writers will talk to you about anything, from their current projects to their sex lives. They will discuss husbands, wives, mates, publishers (especially publishers!) and personal finances with the greatest of candour. And why not? They're so used to laying bare their inner souls and secret selves for the world to see that a one-on-one conversation seems like talking to oneself.

I did observe, though, that for the most part writers write better than they talk. One of the exceptions was a poet who reads her work as beautifully as it's written.

You have to be careful the way you talk to writers. They'll milk you dry of every thought and turn of phrase, and store it away for future reference. They can be discreet, of course, but writers live off words and ideas, and they collect both the way a lake collects water.

This weekend was a rich experience for me. I learned a great deal about a special group of people, and while I've always felt that laying claim to being a writer myself was just a mite pretentious, I did reach this conclusion.

I wouldn't mind being part of that crowd at all.

## Suicide Time

There oughta be a law.

There oughta be a law that does away with all the other laws which allow Lucien Bouchard to be where he is. There oughta be a law that requires the Leader of Her Majesty's Loyal Opposition to take an oath of loyalty to the nation. And finally, there oughta be a law that declares columnists to be national treasures and pays them a six figure salary. Just thought I'd throw that in.

I'm all for freedom of speech. Any dimwitted idiot who has a half-baked idea on any inconsequential issue at all should have the right to talk about his idea to whomever wants to listen. Freedom of speech gives us the right to criticize people in places of authority and decision-making without fear of reprisal. Without free speech, the St. John's city council would have long since sued itself out of existence. Without the guarantee of free speech most married couples would never speak to each other.

What the nation of Canada is giving to Lucien Bouchard has gone way beyond the freedom to speak his mind. We have placed in his hands the equivalent of a loaded shotgun and a licence to kill. To make it still easier for him, we have painted a large bull's eye on the breast of our collective selves. We have placed the barrel of that shotgun flush against that bull's eye and we have said to Lucien, "You may fire when ready, Monsieur. Hopefully, you'll miss."

No other nation on the face of the earth would allow it to happen. It's like inviting your husband's girlfriend to spend the weekend at your house while you're gone to visit your mother and expecting to have a marriage when you get back. It's like allowing the town mutt free access to your prize poodle while she's in heat and expecting to make a good buck selling purebred puppies.

But don't blame Bouchard for taking advantage of the situation, anymore than you'd blame your husband or the town mutt. Bouchard, perhaps the most intellectually gifted politician in Canada since Trudeau, believes passionately in a separate Quebec. Any man of his age capable of talking a beautiful young woman, whom he met on an airplane, into his bed on a permanent basis, is more than capable of taking Quebec out of Confederation. He has a right to those beliefs and a right to act on them within the law. I don't know about the young woman, but he did divorce his other wife and marry this one, so one supposes that he's within his rights there, too. Whatever, this chap has a habit of getting what he wants.

He also has the right, according to Canadian law, to traipse halfway around the globe as Leader of the Opposition and at taxpayer expense convince the rest of the world that a separate Quebec is good for everyone. We're actually paying his expenses, for God's sake! Can you believe it? It's a strange, strange world we live in, Master Jack.

Okay, enough is enough. Something has to be done. Obviously no one in Ottawa has the will to act, so it's left to the common people. That's you and me, and perhaps a few million others. You want to tell your great-grandchildren that you stood idly by while the nation of Canada played Dr. Kevorkian to itself and financed its own death? Me, neither.

Have I got an idea? Is a frog's butt watertight? Listen up, now. I have several possible strategies to lay out. I'll determine by your letters which one you most prefer.

Strategy One. The best defence is a good offence. The other nine provinces and the two territories, by a special act of their legislatures, immediately opt for political union with Quebec. We set up road signs in French (in most cases, we simply erase the English), we buy Celine Dion tapes and we all support the Montreal Canadiens. Okay, perhaps there are some things most of us couldn't stomach, but you get the idea, right? If we're all part of Quebec what can they separate from? By the way, what do you think a separate Quebec would call the Canadiens? The Montreal Quebeckers? The Montreal Separatistes? The Montreal Losers? Anyone's guess.

Strategy Two. Change the laws to make the party with the least number of seats the official opposition on the grounds that the fewer of them there are, the less damage they can do. Please do not protest here that government needs a strong opposition in order to govern effectively. It does, but Bouchard's Blocheads ain't it. Neither is Preston Manning, the chief of defectives. That leaves Elsie and Jean, the odd couple. But at least they're on our side.

Strategy Three (my personal favourite). We all refuse to pay federal income tax until the Bloc is removed from Official Opposition status. It might take an act of Parliament, a quick amendment to the Constitution, a *coup d'état* or all three. But none of us pays a cent until and unless the government acts. You say we'll lose out in federal transfer payments? True. But look what we'll gain in personal income.

We've come to a sorry state in this country when one of our most powerful elected officials is committed to tearing the nation apart and we help finance his dream.

Only in Canada, you say?

Pity.

# Yes, Virginia, There is a Neiman-Marcus Cookie

CBC Radio is a grinch.

You know what a grinch is. In the Dr. Seuss story, the Grinch stole all the presents at Christmas. Today, a grinch is anything or anyone who steals the fun and magic out of anything. CBC Radio is a grinch.

Tens of thousands of you will recall that some time ago I told the story of the lady who got stuck with paying two hundred and fifty dollars to Neiman-Marcus, a department store in the States, for a cookie recipe. She got even by putting the recipe on the Internet and in the papers for anyone who wanted it. Great story. Great cookies, too. There was more than the usual response to a normal column. That week I got two letters, and neither of them from Mom.

Several of you told me you had tried or were about to try the recipe in question. Some of you, the more generous types, even indicated you were sending me a sample. This is as good a time as any to point out that I haven't received anything yet. That, of course, is the fault of the Post Office. Those of you who haven't finished baking should perhaps send my share via Day and Ross.

Some of you will find this next bit difficult to believe but I tell you the truth. Less than a week after my column appeared the CBC Radio grinch took to the airways on a popular afternoon local affairs program. The story, they said, wasn't true. Chuckle chuckle. The whole thing, they said, was a hoax. Heh heh heh.

The recipe, they admitted, was good, but the story was just one of those urban legends that keeps popping up every once in awhile and sucks some well-meaning columnist into believing it. Ho ho ho. Neiman-Marcus doesn't even make cookies. Ha ha ha. And stay tuned for the news.

I told my daughter what had happened—out of earshot of my granddaughter, of course—and she was shocked.

"Blasphemy!" she sputtered. "And on the blessed Sabbath!"

Personally, I am outraged. So outraged that I have decided to take umbrage. How can even a CBC grinch be so insensitive to the need of people everywhere to believe the beautiful and the good? I know CBC has had cutbacks but haven't we all.

Have they had a cut in their belief in miracles? Hasn't anyone at CBC Radio watched a feel-good movie lately? Has *The Little Match Girl* been scrubbed from the late-night movie list? Will there be no *Mary Poppins* this Christmas? No *Nutcracker Suite*? Is the next thing to go *The Ten Commandments* at Easter?

Thousands of happy housewives, thousands of normal house-wives, thousands of women who aren't housewives at all, and thousands of men who'd rather do it themselves have hurried to supermarkets, groceterias, corner stores and confectioneries to purchase Hershey bars and chocolate chips, the prime ingredients of this miracle cookie.

Even as we speak, even as you read, Neiman-Marcus cookies are piling up in their thousands all over the Greater St. John's Metropolitan Area, on the Bald (Bauld? Ball? Balled? Bawled?) Diversion in Corner Brook, on the East Side of St. Anthony, in Forteau and Nain, in Caplin Cove (Hant's Harbour), on Church St. in Grand Falls-Windsor and in my cousin's (older cousin's) house in Kippens. Everyone is baking Neiman-Marcus cookies. And most of them will share with me.

Tell them, CBC grinch, that there are no Neiman-Marcus cookies. Tell them there is no Never-Never Land and no Mickey Mouse. Break some cook's heart this Advent season and tell him or her the cookies do not exist. That the little bags of chocolatey goodness stored in the fridge for Grandpa and Uncle Harry and Cousin Rachel aren't really there because Neiman-Marcus doesn't even make cookies.

No Neiman-Marcus cookies?

Why, CBC grinch, you might as well say there's no Aunt Jemima, no Betty Crocker, no Jolly Green Giant.

No Neiman-Marcus cookies?

You might as well say, CBC grinch, that the Three Wise Men had a road map, that there's no plump little grey-haired idiot who owns Wendy's and makes lousy commercials, that Gandhi invented the sit-in because he flunked out of fencing school.

Of course there are Neiman-Marcus cookies. I have them in a little cookie tin on my counter. Daughter Number Three put them there after she made them. Neiman-Marcus cookies exist just as surely as Scotty can beam me up.

Perhaps the CBC grinch will grin broadly at all this and say, "I do not dispute the existence of the cookies as such, only the fact that they are supposed to be Neiman-Marcus cookies." But that is the same as saying that while we believe in teeth, we do not believe in the tooth fairy. That while we believe in babies, we do not believe in the stork. Or most important of all, that while we would never dispute the existence of Christmas gifts, Santa Claus himself is a matter of some doubt.

Ah CBC grinch, the world is too full of doubters. There are many who will burst the bubble and scorn the magic. And as long as they doubt and scorn they will never know the joy or the fullness of a grated Hershey bar mixed with three cups of chopped nuts and two teaspoonfuls of vanilla.

Is there a Neiman-Marcus cookie?

Yes, Virginia, as long as women purchase Pillsbury cake and cookie mix, as long as men sift and stir, as long as children lick the bowls and steal the spoons, there will be a Neiman-Marcus cookie.

Would the Pillsbury Doughboy lie?

## The Flu From Here

I've got the flu.

Again. I get the flu more often than Brian Mulroney gets the finger.

If it's on the go, I'll get it, sure as there's dirt in a dead duck.

It's not that I'm basically unhealthy, you understand, it's just that I get sick a lot. That's not true. I said it because it sounds cute. It is important in this life to distinguish between what is true and what simply sounds cute. This applies particularly to one's dealings with the opposite sex, especially when they're not as opposite as they used to be.

Actually, I haven't been in a hospital since I was sick—er, six. Six years old, that is. And if my appendix hadn't blown apart at the time I wouldn't have been there at all. Of course, if dear old Dr. Olds hadn't been in Twillingate at the time I wouldn't be here today at all. But I wasn't sick.

Apart from always having the flu, I'm as healthy as a horse, if horses have migraines. But let's forget about that. Please. It's been some time since the last headache and I wouldn't want to bring one on by just thinking about it.

To be honest, I also have athlete's foot. Can't wear nylon socks at all. But that's about it.

It's the flu that is my special nemesis. Deep down I believe I'm allergic to it. Some people get the flu and it never seems to bother them. I come within spitting distance of a virus and I'm immediately stricken and immediately disowned by all who love me. I'm told I'm not easy to live with when I'm sick.

I'm even more allergic to people who claim they never get the flu at all. I have an instinctive dislike for such people, even when such people are my close friends.

"I never get the flu," said a friend who phoned when I was laid low the other day. "No, b'y. Don't know what it is to get the flu."

What are they trying to prove when they put you down like that? I'm miserable enough as it is without this Job's comforter and his smug little comments. What's he trying to say, anyway? That because he never gets the flu he's better than me? Stronger? Healthier? Closer to God?

I mean, you don't go up to someone with leprosy and proclaim, "Never get leprosy myself, you know."

I always look such people over carefully to see if there's something nasty they have that I don't and never will, but it isn't easy. The best I could manage with my friend above was to say with as much condescension as I could muster:

"Well, I've never been under six feet tall," which he is, considerably.

When I told the same chap one day that I had had a migraine headache the night before, he immediately responded with, "You know, I've never had a headache." And when I then told him that I had a royal pain in my buttocks and he was it, he actually started to say, "You know, I've never had a ..." and caught himself just in time.

Sometimes in such situations you just have to let fly with the best you have and hope you hit the nail between the eyes. I've got one response I'm saving for the right moment and just the right person: "I've never had a venereal disease myself."

Obnoxious friends are only one of the problems with the flu. Another is that you have the damn stuff for weeks before you know what's wrong with you. You feel like you have both feet, one hand and the other arm up to the elbow in the grave. Flu is the last thing that comes to mind.

I must be burned out, is your first thought. I'm stressed, that's it. I need more fibre in my diet. Got to get more sleep. Should have had my eyes examined last year. Perhaps it's tooth decay. Or laziness.

Then some close friend points out the obvious.

"Looks like you got the flu. Never get the flu myself, you know." Bang.

Another thing about influenza, to use its full perditious name, is that it never happens to you when nothing else is happening to you. Know what I mean? It's like your car after you get a hundred thousand klicks or so on it and things start giving out. Ever notice that your muffler never falls off in the driveway? That your fuel pump never stops pumping within a hundred miles of the house? That the electronic ignition never gives out in your province?

No sir. These little things happen in the middle of Crooked Bog in a blizzard, or halfway down the Burgeo road at three A.M., or on the 401 in a traffic jam in a heat wave.

The flu is something like that. It only strikes when you have other things to do. I get incapacitated when we're a day away from leaving to visit my daughter in Boston. When I have three seminars to give in one week. During Christmas. The long weekend we had planned to go to the cabin. When OH and I have planned a second honeymoon for some Saturday night. She says I get it on purpose, whenever something important is coming up. Whatever, I can't recall the last time I had a month or so with nothing to do and nowhere to go and got the flu at the same time.

But at least I never give in enough to go to my doctor with my problems. The last thing I would ever do is drag myself to his office complaining of symptoms and general misery. Because I know exactly what I'd hear.

"Got the flu? Never get it myself, you know."

## Roadkill

"Driving Highway Newfoundland is hazardous to your health."

In hunting season there should be a fifty-foot high neon sign to that effect every ten kilometres along every road in the

province, gravel and paved, accompanied by sirens, bells and whis-
tles.

Or they could erect a smaller sign every five hundred metres
saying simply "No hunting for moose along the highway." I'd be
satisfied either way.

Other Half and I drove across the island last Saturday.
Saturday, as you may know, was the first day of the big game
hunting season. That we made it to the City of John's in one
piece is a miracle right up there with the feeding of the five thousand.

I am now convinced that ninety-nine point nine per cent of the
total idiot drivers in this province wear red caps and orange vests
and for the most part, drive pickup trucks. Each truck has a min-
imum of five people in the single seat cab. The driver is squashed
over to the left so much it's not normally possible to see him
through the rear window of the cab.

We caught most of the action from about ten in the morning
to noon. By that time, unsuccessful hunters were tired, frustrated
and seeing double. Since daylight they had been walking the bogs
and searching the woods roads. Chances are they hadn't seen a
thing. Quite possibly they had met at least one hunter spattered
from toe to topknot with the blood of his kill, and that wouldn't
help their dispositions at all.

Now, here they are on the way home to explain to the mrsuses
that there are more moose up their sou'west portion than in these
parts. But with the hope that springs eternal in the human breast,
and often elsewhere, they are keeping their eyes on the bogs and
marshes and burned-over areas by the side of the highway, just in
case.

The problem is twofold. One, it is not possible to keep one's
eyes on the road and on the bogs at the same time. Secondly, by

now the eyes are so tired that they see moose around every bend. Every stump, every small dark boulder, every pile of dirt assumes the configuration of a large hairy animal with antlers. And every few moments, one of the hunters seeing such an apparition cries hoarsely "Moose! Moose!"

No hunting driver this side of Purgatory has the presence of mind in this situation to first put on his signal lights, then slow gradually and pull safely off the highway. The knee-jerk reaction is immediately to slam on the brakes and try to see what his buddy thinks he saw.

Now, if you are the unfortunate soul who happens to come up behind this crew just as the look-out shouts "Moose!" you'd better have a couple of knee-jerk reactions of your own. If you're not quite close enough to see the tell-tale red caps, or if the boys aren't wearing their headgear at the time and you haven't twigged to what's in front of you, you can find the front part of your vehicle suddenly sitting in the pan of a pickup truck.

Last Saturday, I came close on a couple of occasions to involuntarily mating my vehicle with a couple of mobile hunting machines. I mean, there's absolutely no warning. You're driving along happy enough, given the world and all that is therein, and suddenly you're staring up the exhaust pipe of a fellow who a moment ago was five car lengths ahead of you.

After a few close shaves, of course, even the dullest among us get smart and stay our distance. You see the brake lights come on and you have lots of time to slow yourself while swearing at the fools in front of you as a matter of principle. You cautiously pull over to the other lane to go around the numbnut who still doesn't know you're in the world. Lots of time before the next curve to pass someone who's almost stopped, right?

Uh-uh. Let's rejoin the happy group in the pickup cab.

The cry of "Moose! Moose!" echoes above the squeal of the tires skidding along the pavement. The driver is standing on the brakes and scanning the territory in every direction except straight ahead and straight behind. Then just as the truck is almost stopped, the eagle-eyed Hiawatha who raised the alarm, settles back in his seat and says calmly, "Naw, b'y, that was only a black stump now that I comes to see it."

The driver says a fervent "Manure!" and sick of being disappointed yet again, stomps on the gas with the same kind of energy that he used on the brakes and the truck leaps ahead like a startled deer.

Back to you. You are about broadside to the one-ton 4X4 with the V10 engine and coming up fast to the next turn when you realize that the boy behind that other wheel has gone into overdrive and the two of you are roaring side by side down a two-lane road with nothing between you except a double line.

Suddenly, the hunting driver turns and spots you on his port bow. His face turns into a snarl and one middle finger jabs upward and outward in your direction.

"You damn fool," he is clearly shouting, "are you trying to get us all killed, passing on a curve?!"

Now you have a decision to make. Drop back before you lock horns with a twenty-two wheeler, or call the bugger's bluff. Your decision is made for you when you hear the siren and see the red and blue lights in your rear-view mirror.

"But Officer, it was a moose hunter and he slowed down and then he speeded up and I got caught trying to pass him and ..."

"Yeah," says the cop, handing the ticket through the window.

"Bloody nuisances. You watch out for them now."

# The Sweet Smell of Revenge

Everyone knows about the love life of the average American. We see it every day on television. *The Young and the Restless, As the World Turns, All my Children* and a dozen more soaps with the one theme. Sex, sex and more sex.

Americans have sex lives that seem to be in permanent overdrive, people who can never get enough, always hopping into bed with someone else, generally someone else's spouse. Whoop-de-do! Let the good times roll!

The soaps leave little to the imagination, but what they do miss we can pick up in graphic detail on the talk shows. So we have this recurring picture of what it's like to be younger than ninety in America today—glorious, frequent, uninhibited, never-ending sex. Right?

Not hardly. According to the most recent survey of love and life American style—the most complete and accurate since Kinsey, they say—that ain't the way it is at all. The crowd south of the border have been feeding us a very long line.

According to this survey released a couple of weeks ago, rocks—igneous, metamorphic and sedimentary—have a more exciting love life than our southern neighbours. You may have already heard some of the details.

The vast majority of Americans remain faithful to their mates, which is nice. The majority of Americans make love only once or twice a month, which is a bit surprising. The majority of Americans don't go in for the kinky stuff, which is neither here nor there. And the biggest shocker of them all? The survey discovered many prime-of-life Americans have sex only once or twice a year, and sometimes not even that.

Well, knock me down and call me celibate. Will wonders never cease?! You mean to tell me that the soap operas aren't the real thing? That Americans don't spend half their waking lives intertwined with someone else's limbs? That those weirdoes we see on *Springer* and *Geraldo* and *Jenny Jones* who will couple with anything outside the insect world, aren't representative of the average American adult? How are the mighty fallen!

I was thinking about this yesterday while listening to a radio commentary on the American occupation of Newfoundland during World War II and most of the Cold War. The commentator was speculating that having several thousand virile young Americans around didn't do a lot for the average Newfoundland male.

It was suggested that the Yanks emasculated our young men, meaning, as if you didn't know, that their presence had a tendency to weaken Newfoundland manhood, especially in the eyes of Newfoundland womanhood. It's difficult not to agree.

The average young Newfoundlander of the day kept his hands in his pockets, scuffed his boots in the dirt, didn't always have all his teeth, didn't always have all his marbles, didn't add "ing" to his verbs and misplaced his *H*'s something awful when he spoke at all, which was as little as possible to women. To top it all off, he usually didn't have enough coppers in his pocket to buy a girl a stick of gum.

The girls didn't have a problem with this while it was all they had. But then along came the friendly invasion! Picture, if you don't remember, thousands of handsome, virile, clean-cut, young American lads: resplendent in their crisp new uniforms; their even, white teeth; their crooked smiles that would charm the chrome off a car bumper; their softer, slower speech; and their ability to say just the right thing to already throbbing female hearts. And the Yanks had more money in their pockets than most Newfoundland boys had in their dreams.

Truth is, it's difficult to blame the women, given the circumstances.

The local boys never had a chance. Some twenty-five thousand Newfoundland women and more were spirited away by these bold young warriors from another world. And the locals could only seethe in silent rage, helpless to do anything about it except beat the living you-know-what out of any US serviceman who deserved it. Some did, although most were pretty decent fellows who were just a long way from home.

Where am I going with this? I have to draw you a picture?

Okay, keep in mind the results of that American sex survey. Now remember similar surveys done by *Maclean's* magazine on life and love in Canada. Are you with me here? Exactly. Those very accurate and historic *Maclean's* surveys showed Newfoundlanders to be the greatest lovers in all Canada for five years in a row!

How's that for a bunch of disenfranchised and emasculated young Newfoundlanders, eh?

Question is, what on earth happened to all these potent and masculine Americans after they went home? Talk about your deflated image!

We can only imagine the current feelings of thousands of American wives who, after learning the heights to which Newfoundlanders have risen in the last few years (ten times a month on the average, wasn't it?), can only squirm in the same silent frustration which marked the local young men whom they spurned so long ago. So who's sorry now, eh?

Newfoundlanders aren't the type to gloat. We suffered in silence when the Yanks took our girls, and we bask in silence in our newly recognized physical prowess. Of course we do.

Still, perhaps we could be forgiven if the words of a popular American song of a few years ago spring unbidden to our minds and to our hearts and to our lips. We might even be forgiven for humming a few bars as we get ready to retire to our beds for the night. Heck, shall we sing it? Certainly!

Right out loud now, all together:

"Ha ha ha, who's got the last laugh now?!"

## A Christmas Tale for the New Year

You've probably heard this story before.

No, it has nothing to do with Neiman-Marcus cookies. This was a miserable old cuss who thought it was cute to fill the stockings of his two little boys with horse manure. You think that's farfetched? I know of at least one instance where parents put coal in the stocking because the child hadn't been "good." And no, it wasn't me. My parents were not that cruel.

This isn't the prevailing wisdom, but I think it's absolutely atrocious to link the goodness and joy of Christmas to the normal behaviour of little children.

*You'd better watch out, you'd better not cry ...*

Lord, I remember as a small child trying so hard the last few weeks before Christmas not to cry, no matter what the cause. You could have extracted my teeth one by one with pliers and I wouldn't have wept. You could have made our small Newfoundland pony, Blondie, into glue before my very eyes and I wouldn't have shed a tear. Santa didn't bring you anything on Christmas if you weren't "good." Why, he flew right on over your house with miles to spare if you so much as whimpered.

*He's making a list, and checking it twice ...*

Surely there was never a more unconscionable message given to little children than in this song. Santa Claus came across to my child's mind as being as bad as God. Well, perhaps not quite as bad as God. Santa only ignored you if you were bad. God sent you to everlasting hell's flames.

Truth was, both Santa and God loved you only if you were good. I have to tell you this wasn't a comforting thought if you were seven years old and your name was Eddie Smith. I knew there was hardly a soul in the community who would vouch for me. They'd seen me "at it" all year. God help me if Santa Claus went looking to them for a reference on me. And God wasn't likely to be much help, either, given his preference for "good" children and heathen. I didn't fit into either category, although my mother often called me the latter.

How large a step is it, do you think, from believing that neither Santa nor God loves you if you're bad, to wondering how your parents feel about you under the same circumstances? If you have small children, for their sake and yours, don't link crying and "goodness" to either your love or the real spirit of giving, which is the basic message of Christmas. I'm for putting that dreadful song to a match.

Now, where was I? Ah yes. The lovely gentleman who put horse manure in his sons' stockings. You can imagine the scene on Christmas morning.

The first little fellow tore open his stocking with breathless anticipation and then recoiled in shock. He couldn't believe his eyes or his nose. Disappointment overwhelmed him and he started to cry. Softly at first, and then with the anguished sobs of a small child.

The second little chap, like his brother, reached into his stocking expecting to find something exciting or at least delicious, and came out with a fistful of manure. I don't know if you've ever held a bare fistful of manure but it isn't a pleasant feeling. And yes, I do speak from experience.

The boy sat back on his haunches. He stared at the manure for several moments. And then he jumped to his feet and started running around the house, looking into this room and that. He rushed outdoors and ran around the house and into the woodshed.

The first boy ran after him, wiping his eyes. He caught up with his brother as he rounded the henhouse, still on the run.

"Wait," he cried, "what are you doing?"

"I'm looking for our Christmas present," the brother replied breathlessly. "Come on and give me a hand."

"Christmas present? What Christmas present? All we got in our stockings was horse poop. There isn't any present."

"But there is!" his little brother insisted. "Don't you see? With all that manure there just has to be a pony around here somewhere!"

"That's stupid," was all the first boy said and he moped around the house the rest of the day, speaking to no one. But his brother was sure that somewhere close by there just had to be the horse he had always dreamed of, and he spent the entire day combing the area looking for it, excited beyond words.

A lot of people in this province are finding manure in their stockings this Christmas and New Year. The manure comes in the form of a letter or a pink slip indicating that your job is gone or your pay is cut or your EI has run out or your small business is in trouble or there won't be an inshore fishery again next year. Sometimes it's illness or worse. Manure comes in many varieties.

We don't usually have a lot of choice about the manure in our lives. But we do have a choice in how we react to getting it. We can spend the time crying or we can go looking for ponies.

Sure, you say, but what's the point? The little guy's pony existed only in his mind. He would never find it. Think of the disappointment when he realized that. Okay, but ask yourself who got the most out of that day—the boy who spent it crying, or the fellow who spent it searching? No contest, right? Right. And who's to say he didn't find his pony? Perhaps the searching itself made him feel better. We do know his brother found nothing except misery.

Robert Louis Stevenson once wrote that it is better to travel hopefully than to arrive. It's more rewarding to search for something positive, even if it's only in your mind, than to lie down and give in to the bad.

The New Year doesn't look bright for many of us. But in the hard old times of the past when Newfoundlanders got hit with flying manure, they always responded by searching for ponies.

That's why we're still here.

## A Thought or Two

There are only two questions this time of year.

Just before Christmas it's the second most irritating query in the civilized world: "Ready for Christmas yet?"

Okay, you want to know the most irritating question of them all? Easy.

"May I tell him who's calling?"

It isn't a question. It's a demand and it has to do with power trips. But I understand that secretarial schools now tell their students this is an inappropriate and even rude question as a rule, so that particular war is over. Still a battle or two to be fought in isolated areas, but generally it ain't done anymore. If employers listened to their secretaries, it wouldn't happen at all.

Am I ready for Christmas? I don't know. I've had Other Half's present for eight months, which has got to be a new world record for husbands as a species. Is that being ready? Is that what they're asking?

I have strong doubts that the people who ask the question mean it in a religious sense, and most of us would probably resent it if they did, but isn't that rather important?

A more practical question would be "Do you have any money left at all?"—the implication being that if you do, you're probably not quite ready. Applying that criterion, I have to say that I am ready.

After the Big Day, the question most often asked by people in search of meaningful conversation is "What'd you get for Christmas?" There are other variations on the theme such as "Was Santa good to you this year?" and "Hope you didn't get any coal in your stocking!" but the thought is the same.

The whole idea seems to be that the success of the season has to do largely with the amount of aftershave lotion and socks received.

But you know something? No one has ever asked me what I gave for Christmas. No one. Not ever. Which, given that the season has to do with giving, strikes me as passing strange.

And if someone did ask, I wonder how I'd answer. Let's see, now. OH chooses most of our gifts, but I'm not totally removed from the process. We gave perfume to this one and boots to that one and Fruit of the Looms to someone else. Gave quite a bit, actually. When it comes to Christmas, I'm no grinch.

To whom did we give? You say that's more important than what we give? Okay. Well, mostly to family and friends. People who are important to us. Anything wrong with that? Don't go getting high and mighty with me, friend. We put a can or two in the food bank basket and I'm always dropping change in those Christmas kettles.

What percentage of my Christmas gifts is to people in desperate need? I don't know, really. Never thought of it that way. Not very high, I guess. Not compared with what we give to the kids.

Look, it's Christmas. We're supposed to be merry and happy and enjoying ourselves. Why do you have to bring up starving children and poverty-stricken families and homeless old people? This is no time to be making people feel guilty. You're spoiling the day, that's what you're doing. I work darned hard for what I get and there's nothing wrong with giving my family the things they deserve.

Yes indeed. I have the distinct feeling that should anyone ask me what I gave for Christmas, I might get a mite defensive. So might we all.

It reminds me of the story I heard the other day of the old minister who got up before his congregation on Christmas Day.

"My sermon has three points," he said, "and I want to list them for you.

"First, on this day when even the poorest of you have relatively so much in the way of gifts and food, I want to remind you that two thirds of the world's children went to bed hungry last night.

"Second, most of us who like to call ourselves Christian don't really give a damn about the hungry and the homeless.

"And third, most of you down there in your pews are more upset that I said 'damn' in church than you are about the fact that two thirds of the world's children will go to bed hungry again tonight."

You think there's any chance at all in this season of love and giving that we may have our priorities a bit mixed up?

It's just a question.

## "Dear Santa"

Dear Mr. Claus:

Season's Greetings!

I trust you are having a pleasant and relaxing Christmas, and that you were very good to yourself. I am writing to tell you what I got for Christmas and how I plan to put it to use.

My brand new son-in-law (SIL) gave me a hammer. He knew I needed a hammer because it was he who broke my old one. It happened last August when we were extending on my cabin deck in preparation for his wedding to Daughter Number Two.

Trying to haul a ten inch spike out of a plank with a little wooden-handle hammer is not recommended in any carpentry book that I know. To give credit where credit is due, however, he did give me the new hammer.

So did Daughter Number One's fiancé (F#1) who was obviously trying to take advantage of a rather sensitive situation.

Negotiations are underway to get SIL and F#1 back on speaking terms.

I guess SIL sort of forgot that he knocked my Coleman gas lantern over the head of the wharf one night in September when we were cleaning a few paltry tomcods. Fortunately, the tide was way out and the lantern landed in only an inch or so of water. Unfortunately, the inch or so of water was on top of a ton or so of rocks.

Anyway, Mr. Claus, I plan to use the hammer to rebuild my little wharf next summer. My splitting table sits on it and my boat is tied up to it so you can see how important the wharf is for someone trying to get a rounder or two for the winter. The hammer will come in quite handy in wharf repairs, and since I now have two hammers SIL will be allowed to help.

My father gave me a cast net which he had a fisherman knit especially for me. I've always wanted a cast net, especially in June when the caplin are running and I'm up to my rear in the frigid Atlantic trying to net a few with an onion sack tied on to the end of a spruce stick.

A scattered chap with a cast net walks up and down the beach making a cast every now and again, just for bigness. Occasionally he deigns to drop a load in front of a bunch of hangashores standing there with little white pails and plastic shopping bags and pitiful looks on their faces.

Most people humbly accept these handouts, scravelling in the sand like mad dogs, and go home pleased with the world as they know it.

Not me. I wander the shoreline until after dark with my sack and my spruce stick, dashing into the waves here, falling on my bum there, until I get enough caplin to dry a few for my poor parents and my poor self. Pride does have its drawbacks.

Years ago when caplin were thicker than Geritol bottles at a senate committee hearing, a spruce stick and onion sack were fairly effective. Today, when caplin aren't much thicker than PCs at a Liberal fundraiser, it just don't work at all. But with my own cast net, Mr. Claus, I can now cast enough caplin in a week or two for bait for a day's handlining for codfish in the fall—for my own personal use, of course, as the new regulations dictate.

Daughter Number Three gave me one of those newfangled, self-charging, waterproof, shockproof and idiot-proof lights that on a clear night can bounce a beam of light (the "spot") from my cabin in St. Patrick's off a cliff ten miles out the bay. This light is to complement the searchlight that my father gave me last year which plugs into the boat's battery and can bounce a spot off the Rock of Gibraltar. The latter is to help me navigate safely in to the wharf after dark, and the former to get me up the wharf and into the cabin without serious mishap, like falling headfirst over the wharf. Both will be indispensable to my pursuit of the fishery next summer—for my own personal use, of course.

OH gave me a new Coleman lantern simply to take the pressure off SIL and because SIL's wife, my daughter, put her up to it.

OH also gave me a fishfinder, one of those electronic gadgets that tell you how deep the water is and how far off bottom you are, which if you're lucky are one and the same thing. It's also supposed to tell you if fish are lurking underneath your own bottom, hence its name. So you cruise around with your fishfinder scouring the ocean underneath your craft, and when it strikes fish a little "beep" goes off and you simply lower your lines and haul away. Nothing to it.

I'd feel very good about my new fishfinder were it not for the fact that a friend has had one for three years and in that period of time has managed to land, to my certain knowledge and that of his wife's, a total of six codfish.

The interesting thing is that without the help of his fishfinder at all, and indeed without the help of any navigational aid, my friend has managed to find most, if not all, of the barely submerged rocks in Green and Badger Bays. The resultant "beeps" in such "findings" emanate from my friend rather than the fishfinder and come regularly and with some emotion, again according to my friend's wife. I've never been fishing with him myself. I have my own troubles.

So you see, Mr. Claus, I'm pretty well fitted out for the "for-your-own-use" fishery next year. I have hammers, wharf, cast net and lights. I have a fishfinder. There's just this one little thing that you didn't do and now it's too late for Christmas. But I do have a birthday coming up in September.

Could you please send me some fish?

## The Age of Enlightenment

I have been searching for enlightenment.

Ever since the Quebec referendum and the World Series, I have been looking for some sign that this world is ready to move beyond old prejudices and tired traditions, and into the knowledge and reality of the nineteen nineties. It's been a long search. It's easier to find a copy of "The Maiden's Prayer" in a house of ill repute.

Aha, you say, if it's examples of enlightenment you're looking for, my son, I know where not to look for it. Oh? And pray tell, where would that be? Aha, you say again, politics and government. You'd be wasting your time to look for enlightenment there, right? Aha, I reply, wrong.

That's right, wrong. Government is exactly where I found enlightenment of the finest kind. I found the same thing in myself, but more of that later.

Let me hasten to add that it wasn't our government in which I found the enlightenment. This is not to say, of course, that it isn't there. It's just that I haven't been able to find it. Perhaps I don't know where to look. Perhaps it's extremely well hidden.

The government of which I speak at the moment is either in Belgium or the Netherlands, I'm not sure which. It doesn't matter, except to them. Anyway, here's what they did. Seems their Social Services Department had this young man who was mentally disadvantaged, as they say today, but on top of that was also saddled with a strong and rather aggressive sex drive. The fear was that, not being responsible for his actions, he might someday lose control and sexually assault someone. Social workers will tell you this is not an uncommon problem, but this particular Social Services Department had a rather uncommon solution.

They paid him forty dollars a week to hire a prostitute to come in on a regular basis to help him cope with his problem. I am so telling you the truth. Surely you saw mention of it in the local press.

Like you, I was at first appalled. Surely this could not be happening in an enlightened and sophisticated society. They must be out of their minds, I thought. That's taking advantage of the weak and defenseless. Where on earth would they find a prostitute willing to work for forty dollars a week? But I thought some more and realized that with the recession and all, you know, it just might happen. Who am I to judge and all that?

Economics aside, you have to admit that it's a novel resolution to a perplexing problem. And before you jump all over it with righteous hysteria, think about it a bit. There were several alternatives.

The first, and the one adopted by most of us, would be to do nothing and wait until someone got raped or killed and then put the poor fellow away for life. Two victims for the price of one. We would say that nothing could have been done to prevent it, it's too bad and all that, but that's the way it is.

The second alternative would be to simply lock him up "just in case" he committed a crime. But fortunately the law doesn't let us do that. Otherwise there'd be more than a few of us behind bars right now.

A third lovely option would be to castrate the gentleman in question. The authorities admitted to considering that idea at first. But if we're talking ethics and morals here, castrating a human being is, in my view as well as theirs, a long ways down the totem pole from simply purchasing a sexual outlet. I don't even like to see animals fixed.

The fourth alternative was the one they chose, and with it they accomplished three things at once. First, they gratified this person's legitimate if powerful sexual urges. Second, they removed the potential for some innocent third party being hurt. And third, they encouraged small business. You are aware, are you not, that in those parts prostitution is legal?

Back to me and my own enlightenment. A few weeks ago, I wrote a powerful and insightful piece on aging. The column ended with the suggestion that, if all else failed in coping with aging, the thing to do was to run away with a younger woman. I thought that advice was right up there with Horace Greeley's famous admonition to "Go West, young man, go West."

Would you believe that I was accused of writing a sexist column? Absolutely. A friend in Deer Lake wrote and told me off about it. Being a friend and a nice person, she did it nicely, but she did it. She also copied her letter to everyone on the West Coast, so I'm making my reply public.

Her *coup de grâce* (French for "Gotcha!") was the question, "Would you advise me to run off with a younger man?"

Now I try to answer all questions directed to me and I've been giving that one some thought. After great deliberation, and not a few sleepless nights, I have come to the conclusion that yes, I would so advise, if you feel the need and if a suitable candidate comes along. Definitely. Now am I forgiven?

As to being sexist, of course *The View* is sexist. OH tells me so, my daughters tell me so and one of our better women poets told me so. What I write is often sexist.

But knowing it is the essence of enlightenment.

## One Ringy-Dingy

The phone rang the other night.

It has a habit of doing that, perhaps because it's hooked up to Newfoundland Telephone and our number is in the book and all that. I'd be just as happy if the damn thing never rang again. I'd have far less stress. I'd be even happier if we could avoid using it ourselves. We'd have far more money.

Anyway, the telephone rang. Without preamble or prologue a male voice on the other end had a question.

"Does anybody live on the Funks?"

For those of you perusing this from other lands and climes, "The Funks" is a bleak rock in the North Atlantic Ocean off our east coast, home to several thousand seabirds. It is a totally inhospitable place, and to my knowledge no human has ever spent more than a night on it, if that.

When my father finds himself completely disgusted with the world as he sees it, which is not all that infrequent, he is inclined to pronounce, "Just as soon be living on The Funks." It is an expression of total disgust in terms of what the good life should be about. I trust you have the picture.

We are not strangers to weird telephone calls. It's one of the rewards for having your name plastered over a newspaper or two on a regular basis. One of the more interesting of these was from a rather irate lady who let me know in somewhat colourful language what she thought of my tongue-in-cheek comments about Brother Oral Roberts.

The call began with, "Who the f%$# do you think you are?"

Actually, I hadn't thought much about it so I let her continue in the hope that she'd have something enlightening to offer on the topic. She did.

"I am a faithful follower of Brother Roberts," she said strongly, "and compared to him, you're a miserable son of a #$%@%. Brother Roberts is a Christian, like me, and you have no $#%#@%$ business making fun of him!"

Then she hung up. Brother Roberts would no doubt be pleased with her support if not her language.

Actually, it was Other Half who took the Funks call, as it's come to be known. I don't like answering the phone because it invariably leads to trouble. Never have I answered the phone and had someone offer me money or tell me that I had won some marvellous award. To be honest, I have had encouraging and pleasant calls from people who liked something I've written, but these are not so frequent that I wouldn't haul the whole bloody apparatus out of the wall if I had the intestines.

"I beg your pardon?" OH was understandably perplexed.

"Is this Ed Smith's house?"

"Yes, it is."

"Okay. Is anybody living on The Funks?"

The question is roughly analogous to asking if there are any virgins living in the Playboy Mansion.

"Excuse me?" OH was still a bit up in the air on this one.

The caller was getting a bit frustrated himself.

"Look, my wife and I are having an argument about it and I want to know if there's anybody living on The Funks."

"I don't think so," OH replied. "In fact, I'm sure there isn't. No one has ever lived on The Funks. But why are you asking us?"

Natural question when you stop and think about it.

"Well, we have one of these phones where the number shows up if someone calls when we're not in, and The Funks is where it came from."

Incidentally, I consider that particular advance in the communications industry to be right up there with the development of Agent Orange. It's the greatest invasion of privacy since the invention of the Peeping Tom technique.

Suppose you want to call someone without letting them know where you're calling from? Suppose you're at the girlfriend's house and you want to call home to tell your wife you're working late? Or vice versa? Can't be done.

You can't call your boss from a wilderness fishing camp to say you're in Corner Brook working with a client for a couple of extra days. You can't call your spouse from Gander on the way home and say you've just left St. John's, to see if you can surprise her with another man. I know a chap who did that just for the hell of it and got the surprise of his life, not to mention hers. They aren't together anymore.

I trust you're aware there is a code you can use when phoning another number to short-circuit the process. Simply push *67 before you dial the number and you'll have the anonymity you deserve. You're welcome.

But suppose you forget? Or you push the wrong button? Or the thing doesn't work the way it's supposed to? Then, my friend, you could have big trouble.

Where were we? Ah yes. The Funks. OH was more than confused at this point.

"You got a call from the Funk Islands?"

"Yes," said the man, "we certainly did. The call came in while we were out and naturally we called back to see what they wanted. When this woman answered the phone, she said, 'This is The Funks.' 'The Funks?' I asked. 'Yes,' she said, 'The Funks.' Then I asked her what she wanted with us and she said she was your daughter calling you, and she had dialed our number by mistake. So that's why I called you to find out who's living on The Funks."

It was suddenly all clear. OH was almost in hysterics, but she did manage to explain to the gentleman in question.

Our daughter, who lives in Marystown, is married to a chap named Funk.

# Inquiring Minds
# Want to Know

Everything you ever wanted to know about anything.

*Discover* magazine recently listed ten questions to which scientists still don't have any answers. "How large is the universe?" "How did life begin?" and stuff like that. The kinds of questions we go to sleep wondering about every night.

Anyway, I took a good look at these so-called mysteries, like you would, and discovered I had perfectly logical answers for all of them. It might be that I am genius material. It might be that scientists are looking for the answers in the wrong places—science, for example. You decide.

Here then, are the ten great "unsolved mysteries" of science, completely unravelled especially for you. I need no thanks. I could use some cash.

How large is the universe?

Understand that there is a "known" and an "unknown" universe. The known universe extends from a point slightly east of Signal Hill to a point slightly west of The Overpass. The unknown universe encompasses everything outside that particular area. This can be proven by (a) having a conversation with anyone inside the "known" universe about anything outside it; or (b) talking to anyone in government about anything.

Does chaos rule the cosmos?

Unlikely. Although the evil organization, KAOS, tried for many years to overcome goodness and niceness, Maxwell Smart and Agent 99 were more than a match for them. KAOS, one assumes, died when the television series *Get Smart* went off the air. You may regard that answer as somewhat flippant. To be more serious, no one rules the Cosmo's anymore. The New York Cosmo's of the old North American Soccer League are extinct. Chaos is dead whatever way you want to look at it.

How did life begin?

Viewer discretion is advised on this one, so if you're at all sensitive you should skip to the next question, especially if you're an editor. Bet not one of you will, including the editor. This is an interesting question, with almost as many answers as there are lives. Most life began, as Shakespeare so delicately put it, "betwixt the lawful wedded sheets." Some of us had our humble beginnings on daybeds, or in the back seats of Chevies. I know at least one person who claims to have gotten her start in a dory.

How does one cell become a whole body?

The truth is, most cells don't start out to be whole bodies. They don't start out to be anything because they can't think. They're just little cells with no brains or toenails or anything like that. A little cell doesn't up and decide one day that it's going to become George W. Bush. Of course, if it has no brains it just might decide to do that. Other than that it's pretty well accidental. Some cells grow up to have the body of Arnold Schwarzenegger and the brains of Rex Murphy. Unfortunately, the opposite also happens.

Is there any life out there in the universe?

On earth, if you go in one direction long enough, you will eventually come back to where you started. So if the universe is round, same thing applies. Keep going long enough in the one

direction and you'll end up back here and voila! There we are—
life! Of course, if the universe is square, that idea is shot to hell.

How many people can the earth hold?

This question is so simple I'm surprised it's included in this list
at all. Scientists know the exact number of square kilometres on
the face of the earth, right? So they also know the exact number
of square metres, right? Even I can calculate how many people
will fit into a square metre. Some friends and I tried it. For the
sake of their families, I won't tell who they are. Since there's not
room enough to lie down, you can't stack the bodies heads and
tails.

So standing toe-to-toe-to-toe and belly-to-belly-to-belly, a
square metre should hold roughly twelve reasonably shaped
adults who are behaving themselves—two who are not. Now you
simply do your multiplying and find your answer. Don't include
the oceans in your calculations because people can't stand up in
water that deep.

What is consciousness?

Amazing that no one has figured this out. Even the stunnest
doctor can tell you what unconsciousness is. Consciousness, therefore, is simply the state of not being unconscious. "I am not
unconscious, therefore I am conscious." Me and Descartes, thick
as thieves.

What drives climate?

God, in the rest of the world. In Newfoundland, Satan.

Can we wipe out disease?

Certainly. Unfortunately, it keeps coming back.

Who peopled the planet?

Excellent question, but hardly complete. Which planet? If
we're talking Jupiter or Mars, the answer is relatively simple. No
one. If we mean earth, the answer is equally simple—relatives.

Your relatives and my relatives, our forefathers and our fore-mothers. They were all at it. The result was inevitable—peopling.

If you're interested in other, less interesting answers to these questions, read the November *Discover*. But you already know all you need to know.

## Greetings and Salutations

I dropped into a Wal-Mart store the other day.

Actually, it was Other Half's idea. Something in there she wanted me to see, she said, the perfect gift for Cousin Jeremy or someone. I can't remember who it was. OH is the Santa Claus in this partnership. I don't even get veto rights on costs. Whatever, only Wal-Mart had it, so into Wal-Mart we had to go.

It was my first time, and to be honest a bit intimidating. I felt like a virgin about to be deflowered on the altar of high retail, and believe me it's been a long time since I felt like that—a virgin, I mean. How long? You gotta be kidding.

The name "Wal-Mart" conjures up images of super-sales-people filled with super-energy who are super-friendly and want to sell you super-products at super-prices. Even the act of entering the store is supposed to be a super-experience as you are greeted by this super-warm, super-sensitive person who makes you feel as though she'd rather see you walk through those doors than Tom Cruise naked in the honeymoon suite of a Bahamas resort.

I half expected a symphony orchestra to break out in "Hail to the Chief" as I entered, and nothing less than an assistant manager to come running with gifts and flowers to welcome me into this mecca of retailers, this paradise of shoppers, this little bit of the super-super USA right here in Nufunlund.

You've all heard about Wal-Mart. You probably even know they have cheerleader practice in the mornings. I don't know if they have pompoms and cute girls or not, but ...Well, of course they have cute girls at Wal-Mart. I didn't mean to imply otherwise. I was talking cheerleader cute, fine sexist lout that I am. And ... of course I know that the girls at Wal-Mart are every bit as cute as cheerleaders. Good heavens, people, can't a poor columnist make a stupid little comparison? No, I don't mean cheerleaders are stupid ... Look, can we go on to something else? Thank you.

I am told that at these early morning rah-rah sessions employees have to sing a Wal-Mart song or something, give solid evidence of high energy and exhibit a missionary zeal to get the hell out there and sell, sell, sell as though their jobs depended on it.

I would not make a good Wal-Mart employee. First, I am not a morning person. Second, I do not react well to being rah-rahed. Anyone, therefore, who tries to rah-rah me before nine A.M. is running a fair risk of being cut down like the grass of the field. Even OH doesn't try to rah-rah me in the morning. No telling what would happen if she did, which is probably why she doesn't.

Anyway, we were in this Wal-Mart store for a good three minutes before it hit me with the force of a can of beans up the side of the head that I had not been greeted at the door.

What a disappointment! What a rip-off! One of the eight or ten reasons for coming into this place to begin with was to be greeted. I had heard about it. I was looking forward to it. Visions of scantily clad young women hanging garlands of flowers around my neck and kissing me welcome had been haunting my dreams for weeks. That's Hawaii? Oh. Sorry.

Actually, I had expected it to be better than Hawaii. Better than a geisha leading you into a hot bath. Better than a silk sheet under ...you get the point. And it hadn't happened at all!

Was I upset? Is the health of your cat's urinary tract important? I was so steamed I grabbed OH by the arm and hissed, "I wasn't greeted. I'm getting my money back."

OH looked at me with something less than kindness.

"Might be difficult," she said.

"Why?" I demanded. "I'll see the manager, I'll see the owner, I'll see the greeter, I'll—"

"The major problem," OH pointed out, "is that you haven't bought anything."

I hate it when she's practical like that.

"Besides," OH went on, "perhaps the greeter was busy greeting someone else. Perhaps she was on break. Perhaps she didn't like your looks. Perhaps she read one of your columns."

"Seems an awful waste of money to me," I said, and knew I was being sullen, "to have greeters who don't greet everybody."

By that time OH for some reason or other wanted to leave the store.

"Perhaps," she said over her shoulder and not without a trace of sarcasm, "they'll have someone at the exit to say 'Goodbye' to you."

They did. The woman at the door was into the "Have a nice day" mode and sort of flung it at a group of us who were all leaving at the same time. I don't think she singled me out personally. And it wasn't the same thing as being greeted.

But it didn't matter. Greeters and goodbyers at shopping centres are in the same class as flight attendants who assure me as I make my grateful way off the previously doomed aircraft that they were really pleased to have me aboard this trip. Sure.

Last time I flew, I thought I'd be at least polite and say "thank you," but she was already repeating the line to the drunk behind me.

OH says we have to go back to Wal-Mart sometime before Christmas to pick out a present for someone on her side of the family. I'm not fussy about it, but I suppose I should go.

Everyone deserves a second chance.

## Going Solo

Samantha and I were going to a Christmas skating party together.

Just the two of us, all by ourselves. I explained to Son-In-Law (SIL) that we had only two hours to look at our rabbit snares that afternoon because we had to be back in lots of time for me to get ready.

Samantha is just a year old and this is the first time I've been allowed to take her anywhere myself. Not that I wanted to particularly, you understand. But it's a grandfather's responsibility to do these things so I will do them.

I made sure SIL understood clearly we had to be back from the woods in time to get the baby warmly dressed, even though it meant not being able to look at all our snares or snowmobile as much as we wanted. He didn't look all that happy and I assured him that I was as disappointed as he not to be spending the whole afternoon out in the wide open spaces. But taking Samantha to this party was my responsibility and I meant to see it through.

We were back within the hour because I was afraid we'd get the machines bogged down in the deep snow and someone else would have to carry Sam to the party, someone whose responsibility it wasn't. I have too much pride to let that happen.

I washed, showered, shaved and shampooed as befits a man about to take a beautiful young lady out on the town, and within the half-hour was at SIL's house impatiently waiting to fulfill my obligations. It's what society expects of grandfathers.

Somewhat to my surprise, Daughter Number Two was dressed up and made up and obviously going somewhere. Ah, I thought to myself, taking advantage of the old man looking after the kid to go visit some friends. Well, why not. Part of a grandfather's role is to give the parents a break from the rigours of child-rearing. No problem.

"So where can I get in touch with you if I need you?"

I was thinking primarily of diapers and the need to change them at least once a week. The responsibilities of grandparenthood go only so far as far as this grandparent is concerned. I don't do diapers. I don't do vomit. Been there, done that and got the sick stomach.

"You have only to call if you get in trouble," she said. "But I just changed her diaper and she isn't sick so you've got nothing to worry about."

"Okay, but what number do I call, just in case?"

"Number?" Daughter was obviously confused. "You won't need to telephone me. I'll be right there with you."

"You're coming with us? Why are you coming with us? I was looking forward to—I mean, it's my responsibility to take Sam out myself, to give you a break. We don't need you, especially if you've just changed her diaper."

Daughter tried to explain.

"It's not that I'm coming with you exactly," she said. "Oh, I'll go in the same car and I'll be in the stadium watching, but really, Dad, you're all on your own. By the way, we'll take our car because the child seat is already in it, and I can drive to give you a spell."

It's roughly ninety seconds from her house to the stadium by slow mule.

"Look," I demanded, "what's the real purpose in your coming with us? Is there some reason you feel I can't discharge my responsibilities as a grandparent? Are you forgetting I raised four of you runny-nosed little specimens? Practically every moment of that experience is burned into my brain. There's no way I can forget how it goes."

"I know that, Dad," she said soothingly. "I have every confidence in you to take care of Samantha. I just want to take some videos of you two going out together all by yourselves for the very first time."

Well, all right.

So we got to the stadium. I was introducing Samantha to friends—another onerous obligation—when I heard this voice droning away directly behind me, something like the commentators who cover golf tournaments, not exactly a whisper and not exactly out loud.

"This is Grandfather taking Samantha to the Christmas party at the rink. This is Grandfather talking to some people. This is Samantha looking as if she's going to throw up ..."

It was time for a frank father-daughter talk.

"Look, if you follow me one more foot making silly commentary for that stupid camera, I am going to chuck this responsibility as of right now. I'm not Prince Charles, Sam isn't heir to the throne and you're not photojournalist of the year. Now stop embarrassing me."

"Okay," she said brightly. "And by the way, I put the stroller in the car so you could push Samantha around the ice. Makes her safe and gives you something to hold on to."

We had made a few circuits of the rink, Sam in the stroller and me holding on to it, when she began to get a bit fussy. I looked up to see Daughter hanging over the boards holding out a baby bottle of milk, the way they hand water to marathon runners.

"Samantha's wrist is bare," she said as we careened by. "Haul up her mitten."

Later at home as she was undressing the baby, she said to her husband, "I've got some great shots of Dad and Samantha Rae at the party. Imagine, the two of them going out all by themselves!"

I could be wrong, but I swear Sammy burst out laughing.

## Singalong

Was part of a great singsong the other night.

Perhaps you don't like to sing. In that case, this column is not for you. What I intend to do, you see, is analyze the singsong phenomenon with particular reference to, and emphasis on, those types of individuals who like to take part in it. If you've never been in a good, old-fashioned, rousing singsong you won't relate to this, so frig off and paint the house or something.

On the other hand, if you like to make fun of people there may be something here for you after all.

I've been trying to identify those experiences in life that tend to draw people closer together and make them feel a fellowship and a camaraderie found nowhere else outside a honeymoon. There aren't many. In fact, I found only two.

The first is a good drunk. Say what you like about the evils of drink—and you'd be right, of course—nothing draws people closer together than sharing the contents of a glass of milk, particularly when it's been mixed with Tia Maria. In that regard, I believe the therapeutic effects of alcohol to have been grossly underestimated over the years.

In the words of the poet:

*There's the love of a man, and the love of a wife;*
*There's the love of a father and mother.*
*But there's never a love like the wonderful love*
*Of one old drunk for another.*

I have had occasion to witness (as opposed to being involved in) this love lately and at length and have found it to be an extremely strong devotion.

The only other life experience that comes anywhere close to having the same effect is the singalong. You throw together fifteen or twenty people who have nothing better to do and nowhere better to go, add a guitar and a couple of spoons and you have the makings for one of life's finest offerings.

I have been part of countless such singsongs in my life. They reach their highest form when everyone present loves to sing and is there for that reason only. Some of my most cherished memories are from such times. When you just happen to have a crowd of people sitting around after a conference or at a party and someone just happens to have a guitar and someone else just happens to start singing, the results can range from the sublime to the ridiculous.

The chap with the loudest voice is usually he who can't carry a tune in a handbasket. He often tries to sing harmony, thus creating total musical hell. The people sitting nearest this fellow first try drowning him out. This never works. Then they try changing seats with someone else. This never works, either.

As the evening progresses, however, with the help of a scattered glass of milk, people have a tendency to warm up to this fellow. At a certain point, usually measured in numbers of glasses of milk, no one notices or cares who's singing what and everyone loves everyone else, anyway.

Then there's always the person who keeps trying to sing songs no one has ever heard of before, such as "I've Been Flushed From the Bathroom of Your Heart" and gospel tunes like "Drop Kick Me, Jesus, Through the Goalposts of Life." For some reason unknown to science or Nashville, this is usually a woman. If she's an ordinary participant, no problem. You simply ignore her. But if she's the one with the guitar, pure chaos. She'll sing each of those songs, word for word, while everyone else fidgets.

In desperation, someone will start "On Top of Old Smokey," attracting part of the group. Someone else will get into "Liverpool Lou" and a third group is off on "How Great Thou Art." Meanwhile, Our Lady of the Unknown Song is blissfully unaware of any of it as she croons on into "Love Me or Leave Me the House and the Car."

One of your more interesting singsong types is the fellow who after a drink or two or three wants to get into the dirty songs. With great gusto he leads the group into "Seven Old Ladies Got Locked in the Lavatory" which is usually acceptable, and "The North Atlantic Squadron," which usually is not.

Inevitably, and unknown to him, this chap is sitting next to the wife of the pastor of the Church of the Woolly Haired Sacrificial

Lambs down in Puncheon Gut Tickle, a somewhat fundamentalist group not much given to pornographic renditions of "My Bonnie Lies Over the Ocean." However, you can tell you've got a really great party going if she starts to sing along with him.

Last but not least are those who don't want to sing but don't want to be anywhere else, either. So they get into this earnest conversation about the effects of fog on jockey shorts and try hard to make themselves heard above the singers. They usually do, but they make a lot of enemies in the process.

All that being said, singsongs are like sex. There's no such thing as a bad one. People who sing together create a bond that's thicker than blood and far tastier. You can hear it next morning at breakfast.

"What time was it we got to bed? That's what I thought. We must be nuts. Anyone see Mike this morning? That's what I thought. Great time though, eh?!"

I wish we did more of it.


# The Desensitizing of the Newfoundland Palate


I have to admit to being truly worried.

On the way to or on the way from somewhere the other day, I was listening to the phone-in show *Crosstalk* on CBC Radio. The topic for the day was Newfoundland cuisine, and people were calling in to talk about their favourite ways of preparing marinated sculpin heads and other such local delicacies. It was all very interesting.

But I really gasped and stretched my eyes when someone called in to ask what was surely the most ridiculous question since Saddam Hussein asked George W. Bush if he'd like to come for dinner. What struck me as even more preposterous was that the hosts were taking it seriously.

The question? How do you get the taste of turr off the turr? Or the smell of salt-water duck off the duck? Would you believe it?!

Aha, I said, must be mainlanders, all of them. No Newfoundlander would ever ask such an idiot question. Just wait until a Fogo Islander or a Labradorian gets through on that phone. Then we'll get an earful.

The next caller came in from the West Coast. I listened carefully. Yes, she said, she knew how to get the turr taste off turrs. She always puts an apple inside the turr before baking.

Obviously another mainlander. If you fill up the turr with apples, my dear, pray tell where you put the stuffing? And if you have no stuffing, what's the point of baking a turr? Wait till the real Newfoundlanders get through, I thought viciously. They'll put an end to this foolishness.

Finally this chap came on from the Labrador coast. He was listening to the discussion, he said, and wanted to state his views. Here it comes, I thought, now we're going to hear it. Yes, he went on, most people on the Labrador these days were skinning their turrs and that took away the taste and the smell just fine.

I was absolutely floored! Skin a turr? You might as well throw away the back from a rabbit or the hindquarters off a moose. We're not talking pullets and hens here, people, we're talking turrs! Show me a skinned turr and I'll show you a tasteless turr which, come to think of it, is exactly what buddy from the Labrador was saying.

I guess there's something awfully wrong with me. I thought we ate turrs because we like the taste of turr. I thought we ate salt-water duck because we like the taste of salt-water duck. If after all the trouble it takes to get your mitts on either bird these days, you're going to go through even more trouble to remove the taste, tell me what in hell is the point of having them in the first place?

It was all very sad. Before the show was over, several people had called to give their favourite methods of removing both taste and smell. No one called to say that they left the skin intact, stuffed the thing with dressing, put a few strips of bacon across the breast and let the aroma permeate the house and the yard and the whole cove as nature intended.

The final blow was when someone called to say that they dipped their birds in baking soda to reduce the flavour to neutral.

The whole thing left me dejected and depressed. I can think of no better illustration of the degree to which Newfoundlanders have lost touch with their past and their heritage, and especially their birds.

A few weeks ago I was talking to a fellow who was exclaiming over the marvellous moose he had bagged last fall. I knew he was laying it on deliberately for me because I didn't get one, but suddenly he said one of the stupidest things I have ever heard a moose hunter say, and I've heard some weird ones.

"Some moose, my son!" he declared proudly. "Some moose! Best I ever had. Don't taste like moose atall. Same as fresh beef. The wife cooked a bit the other day and the minister came in just as we was sittin' down to eat, like he always do, and you know what? He wouldn't believe it was moose. Swore up and down, he did, that it was fresh beef. Yessir, best moose I ever had!"

Now that fellow hunted for weeks, left home and family totally neglected for most of the fall, spent enough money in gas and supplies to buy a dozen head of cattle, all to get a moose that didn't taste like a moose.

Is something wrong here? Or am I going senile?

If you have to talk about removing the taste and the smell from the things you eat, I would appreciate a program on how to do it with broccoli or radish or cauliflower or any Lean Cuisine dish. Show us how to neutralize the tang of that stuff and they'll be doing us all a large favour. Or tell us how to get the smell of salt herring out of a Sunday suit, especially on a Sunday.

Personally, I think the whole thing is a plot by the federal government to wean us off the things we most like to eat. That way it'll be easier to move us all out of here to some colourless and bland part of the country such as the Niagara Peninsula or Vancouver Island.

Mark my words, before long you'll be hearing ways to get the taste off codfish and trout and how to keep from smelling rabbit when it's baking in the oven. What else will the federal government try in this vain attempt to tear us from our roots, I wonder? What other devious plans are up their sleeves to divorce us from everything that we know and love? I have to admit to being truly worried.

In fact, I don't like the smell of it at all.

## The Strength of Weakness

I'm not afraid to admit a weakness.

And as it happens, I have one. Claustrophobia, the fear of small places such as elevators. The fear of being in some place you can't get out of when you want to, like an aircraft.

If I had any other weaknesses I'd tell you about them. Honest.

Having a weakness is almost as good as having Tom Cruise looks as far as women are concerned. Women love men who seem vulnerable. Brings out their nurturing side. Wins them over every time. But it doesn't explain OH's initial attraction for me because when we were going out together I didn't have claustrophobia. It's possible I had some other weakness at the time. Can't remember what it was, though. Neither can OH.

I've written about this thorn in my flesh before. I write a column about it every time I fly. Fortunately for the reading public, I don't fly that often.

I was asked to go to Vancouver last weekend to give a couple of lectures and do some after-dinner speaking. It sounds impressive, but I was really their third choice, Lucien Bouchard and Mother Teresa both being unavailable.

In case you're reading this, Mr. Premier, please be advised that the crowd in British Columbia paid for the works. And I took three of my pitifully few annual leave days for the trip. So back off! (Sir.)

There are just three problems for someone like me being invited to beautiful Vancouver: (1) getting there; (2) being there; (3) getting back. We'll deal with each in turn.

The only way to get to BC and back within the same calendar year is to spend nine hours each way cramped up in the economy section of various aircraft, much of the time next to a large matron who has decided that her major purpose in life is to replace the absolute terror in my soul with boredom of equal value. She does, but the change doesn't come easily. I spend the moments before take-off making peace with my Maker and trying to remember which sins are most likely to keep me out of Paradise. It's a lengthy list.

Most of you are aware that the domestic air traveller leaves Newfoundland via Dash-8's. Dash-8's do not have jet engines. Dash-8's have turbo props. Some of the more intense moments of my life have been spent watching those ridiculously tiny propellers clawing frantically at the air in a desperate attempt to get us up off the ground before we ran out of airstrip. By the time we were safely (relative term) in the air, I had confessed to every sin in the book, and a few that the book had never heard of.

Actually, I prefer the little Dash-8 to the great huge 747 which takes off like a V2 rocket and over which I have not the slightest control. In the smaller plane I know that by lifting both feet off the floor and flapping hysterically with both arms I can help get the thing airborne.

If getting to Vancouver is a problem, being there is even more so. Being there means living in a hotel which means having to use elevators to get to your room, unless you want to camp out in the gift shop.

But this time I have been smart. This time I took the trouble to call the hotel in advance and request a room at the bottom. They assured me that the best rooms are on the top floors. The conference organizers would want me at the top, they said.

"Do the rooms at the bottom have a bed?" I inquire.

"Certainly, sir."

"And do they have a toilet?"

"Of course, sir."

"Then put me in a room at the bottom before I call my federal member!"

"Yes, sir!" They've obviously heard of George Baker.

So here I am at the registration desk of this hotel in downtown Vancouver, where I am known and loved by no one, and the desk clerk announces that I am in a room on the fifth floor.

"This cannot be," I say in desperation, "I specifically asked for accommodations on the bottom floor. I even had a sweet young thing from the conference follow it up with alternate reservations for the bottom floor. I want the bottom floor!!"

"The fifth floor is the bottom floor," the clerk explains patiently, "for rooms."

Nothing for it now but to hoof it up and down five flights of stairs.

"Is there a problem with using the stairs?" I ask.

"Certainly not, sir. The stairs are right over there, but the elevators will take you ..."

Never mind the flipping elevators, woman, just show me the flipping stairs. She does. The door to the stairwell is locked solid. How do I get to the stairs? The clerk hesitates.

"We'll have to call security," she says. "I forgot these doors are always locked for the protection of our guests."

"I don't want protection," I tell her, "I want access."

Ten minutes later a harried looking chap arrives in a jangle of keys and wants to know the problem. So I tell him, openly and frankly. Surprisingly, he says he understands. Says he had an uncle who was sick like that, too. The only problem here, he says apologetically, is that he can't open the security door without the permission of the manager.

I point out I don't care if they have to clear it with the premier of British Columbia. Ten minutes later the manager, a strikingly attractive young woman, arrives and wants to know the problem. The clerk tells her. The security chap tells her. I tell her.

"No problem," she says brightly, "let's escort Mr. Smith to his room, shall we?"

So the three of them, each carrying a piece of luggage, walk me up the stairs and to my room.

"Now," says this managerial angel, "anytime you want to use the stairs and need the door unlocked, Mr. Smith, you just call and I'll be there."

No one said having a phobia was all bad.

I used the stairs a total of one hundred and six times in the two days I was there and it was the security chap who turned up every time. But it was without complaint and without delay and they treated me as if I were normal. The only way I can thank them is to identify the hotel, the Vancouver Renaissance.

Problem three? Getting back?

I'm here, aren't I?

## To Each His Own

Tomorrow, July 12, is Tit Day.

Otherwise known as Orangeman's Day. Sometimes referred to by Protestants as "Take a Catholic to Lunch" Day, preferably the same Catholic who took you to lunch on St. Patrick's Day.

I prefer to call it Tit Day. As usual I have my reasons and just as usual, I am willing to share them with you, just as soon as I share with you how much I hate that word "share." Whenever I hear it I want to throw up and take off in the opposite direction from which the "sharing" is coming.

There's always someone who wants to "share" something with you these days. The last time I looked it up, about thirty seconds ago, the word "share" meant to allocate or divide or distribute—good stuff like that. It had nothing to do with telling someone your life's experiences, crying on someone's shoulder or trying to involve someone else in your emotional traumas.

Beware the sentence, "I have something to share with you." They're not talking about bread or wine or body. It's not about money or clothes. You won't get a thing out of this "sharing" business except misery. Fact is, someone wants to unload on you and make you as wretched as they are.

Occasionally, someone wants to "share" what he or she considers to be an inspiring or uplifting experience, usually a repentant sinner, and the odds are good it will be something that (a) makes you exceedingly uncomfortable, like when your soul is involved, or (b) something you couldn't give a fig newton about, like when someone else's soul is involved.

There should be a law against "sharing," except when it has to do with money and clothes and preferably someone else's.

Now, where were we? Oh yes. Tit Day. You're probably wondering about that. You may even be slightly offended, which reminds me: people tend to get offended far too easily these days. Taking offence is our number one pastime. And we're getting so good at it that we can take it from practically nothing and often do. The thing about it is that once taken, offence seems to be extremely difficult to lose or shake off.

I was mortally offended once. The feeling is nothing to write home about. Actually, the whole thing was a mistake and the other person didn't intend to insult me at all. But I was easily offended in those days, being young and stupid as opposed to old and stupid, and took offence where none was ever intended. It was a terrible feeling.

Fortunately, the young woman involved made a point of assuring me that she did not intend to hurt my feelings (she said she always laughed at such moments), and I was so immensely pleased that I gave the offence back to her for immediate disposal and went on my way rejoicing. Who wouldn't, given the grievous feeling of being offended? Beats me.

We were talking about Tit Day, or as it is better known, Orangeman's Day. It's the Protestant's day to howl. The Catholics had theirs back on March 17, St. Patrick's Day. If Catholics had any sense of compromise and fair play at all, they'd call theirs Knights of Columbus Day, just to even it up a bit, seeing as how Protestants don't have any saints to speak of. We could call July 4 St. William's Day, I suppose, but most Orangemen would probably balk at that.

I have always felt that Protestants got the dirty end of the stick on this holiday business. St. Patrick's Day comes in the middle of the school year when everyone is dying for a holiday. When do we get Orangeman's Day? Smack dab in the middle of summer. What lesson are we giving our children here, people? That Catholics deserve a holiday and Protestants don't? Think about it.

Catholics have it all over Protestants in a dozen ways.

Take sin. Protestants worry so much about sin, both before and during the sinning, that they don't enjoy it very much. Consequently they don't do it very well. It doesn't stop us from sinning, of course, but we feel guilty about it even before we do it (understand I am using the royal plural here).

Catholics, on the other hand, are just as concerned about sin as Protestants, but they don't worry about it until after the fact. That way, they can not only better enjoy the sin, enjoyment being what sin is all about, but also they can make a better job of it, not being distracted by premature guilt.

Catholics operate on a principle I have found to be basic to the good life: it is better to ask forgiveness than permission. Catholics are strong on forgiveness. Protestants are strong on guilt. I leave it to you to decide who has the most fun.

Back to Tit Day. Some of you must be wondering just a little why I refer to July 12 as Tit Day. Allow me to explain. Why do you think we have an Orangeman's holiday at all? Because we have St. Patrick's Day, of course. This province would never allow Catholics to have a holiday and Protestants not, or vice versa. What goes for one must go for the other.

It was ever thus. The Catholics build a church, the Protestants build a church. The Protestants build a school, the Catholics build a school. The Catholics start a bingo game, the Protestants start a prayer meeting. Give and take, to and fro, a day for a day. Quite simple, really.

Tit for tat.

## Meeting the People

I am a shoal in a rough sea.

That's what it feels like, sitting at a table at the entrance to Coles bookstore in Corner Brook, autographing my latest book, explaining the title.

"No, Ma'am, it's not *Never Wink with Your Eyes Shut*. It's *Never Flirt with Your Eyes Shut*. There's a world of difference. How do I know? Well, have you ever tried winking with your eyes shut? No? Okay, have you tried flirting with your eyes shut? You have?

How'd it go? You don't know because your eyes were shut? Right you are, Ma'am. Next!"

Human traffic surges around me for four hours, the main stream of it giving me a wide berth. It's as though I'm surrounded by a magnetic field. Or encased in the Cone of Silence. People come walking through the mall in a straight line, suddenly see me there and immediately veer to starboard or port, depending on their direction.

Can't say I blame them. If they come close enough to me and my books they feel a subtle pressure to buy. I try removing it with friendly smiles and come-hither glances, but it's still there. I understand and nods accardin' from a distance.

But a surprising number brave the shoals and the magnetic field and the pressure and stop to say hello. Lovely, most of them.

Among the first are two women who say they are born-again Christians attending a healing mission over at some church and have dropped by for a chat. Uh oh. Born-again Christians make up a large share of those who do not love me well. I brace myself for some gentle—they both look like charming people—chiding.

"We want to tell you how much we enjoy your columns," the first one says.

"And," adds the second, "to say we appreciate the spiritual element we often see in your work."

Well, hallelujah and praise be! I keep telling people that there is such a serious component to my writing, but few there be who believe it. There be fewer still who find it. But these two beautiful souls see what many others miss and make an effort to tell me so. I feel like following them home for Christmas.

A small head peers at me from over the edge of the table. Small boy. He picks up a book and slowly leafs through it, looking carefully at each page.

"Can you read?" I ask doubtfully.

"No," he says, staring at the cover, "but these books look good."

I take an immediate liking to him. My picture is on the cover. Full length.

"How much is this book?"

I tell him the price. His face falls. He picks up another.

"How much is this one?"

I tell him. He turns to a third.

"How much is this one?"

I tell him they're all the same price.

He reflects briefly. "I guess that's because they all say the same thing."

I say that's pretty much the case.

"Are you selling these books?"

I tell him no, Coles is selling them. I'm just signing them for the people who buy them.

"My name is Robert," he says, "and I'm in kindergarten. That's why I can't read."

Then he leaves with a small wave. I truly hate to see him go. And I almost steal one of my books from Coles to give him. I'd sign it "To Robert, for when he can read." But by the time I think of it he's gone.

Not long after a middle-aged man detaches himself from the mainstream and makes his way over with a purposeful stride. He looks as though he hasn't smiled in a decade or two and isn't about to begin with me.

"What are you trying to do to people?" he demands.

Not sure of the answer to that one myself. So I stall for time and ask him what he means.

"You don't write the facts." His voice is accusing and belligerent. "You are deliberately misleading people."

I do a quick scan of his body for baseball bats, pitchforks, or "The Watchtower." Seeing nothing, I get bold. I tell him I write opinion, not fact, and most people have enough sense to know the difference. For some reason this upsets him even more and he tells me he's "had contact" with five different colleges and can I match that. I tell him he's obviously a far better educated person than I, despite strong evidence to the contrary, and he leaves with a disgusted wave of the hand. He does not buy a book.

Okay, Smith, I say to myself, now you've seen both ends of the continuum. Everything else should fall in the middle. Myself isn't quite sure.

Another gentleman approaches, his hands clutching something under his overcoat. Oh God, this one does have a bat or a hammer or an 8 X 10 glossy of Pierre Burton. He sidles up, glancing left and right, and stealthily draws his hand out of his coat. In it is a copy of my book.

"I know I'm supposed to buy your book here for this," he almost whispers, "but I bought this one at another bookstore last week. Would you mind signing it anyway?"

So I do, keeping my back turned so the Coles employees don't see what we're up to and feeling a little like Brutus when he stabbed Julius Caesar.

To make matters worse, at the same moment one of the Julius Caesar people comes by with a cup of coffee and a little tray of sweets "to help keep you going." Talk about your basic guilt trip. But they're like that all afternoon, making sure I'm okay and don't want for anything. Real nice people working at Coles. Better than I deserve. Not really, but a strong dose of humility may be in order here and constitutes the only spiritual element you're likely to find in this particular column.

There are so many others during the afternoon. An old friend who is a delight to see. A relative or two. Several acquaintances. Many nice strangers. And Robert.

God bless Robert.

# First Step Along the Road

Samantha Rae took her first step a couple of days ago.

That may not cause your crank to go into double overtime, but it got her parents in a tizzy. Daughter Number Two about had a fit. Called everyone she knew, a few she didn't and yelled it out the back door for the greater edification of the neighbours.

Son-In-Law said "Cool," which is about as excited as he gets. In fact, he said it twice. "Cool."

Her grandparents? We're a mite more controlled, emotionally speaking. We can sit back and reflect on what that first step leads to, and wonder if we should have allowed it.

It's always been a theory of mine that mankind's first big mistake was in standing up on his hind legs because that left his fore legs, which later developed into arms and hands, free for mischief. You think we would have had two World Wars if we had never gotten up off all fours? Or professional wrestling? Or the St. John's Municipal Council?

What damage could Hitler have done running around on his knuckles? How threatening would Saddam Hussein be standing on three legs to pee? Who'd be worried about the future of Quebec if Lucien Bouchard were a quadruped?

When you think about the damage arms and hands have done to humanity, it's difficult not to feel that we wouldn't have been better off running around with our stomachs low to the ground and our tails up in the air, assuming we had tails, of course.

On the other hand, if our arms had stayed legs we couldn't hug anyone.

We couldn't take one of our young by the hand or teach her to ride a bicycle.

We couldn't write "I Love You" in the sand, except maybe with our toes, and if we hadn't learned to do it with our hands first, our toes could never have done it at all.

Without hands there would be no piano concertos, no violins, no symphonies. Would it matter? Birds don't have hands, but they can make beautiful music. Of course, they do stand on their hind legs.

If we had stayed on all fours as was intended given our anatomy, there would be no swords, no guns, no weapons of mass destruction. Would it matter? Nature is governed by violent death within itself. We've simply refined the process.

But what about Samantha Rae?

At the moment, she's got nothing to do with symphonies or bombs. She uses her little hands to draw herself up, ready to take that next hesitating little step. And when she does, she will inevitably fall and probably cry. Someone will pick her up and wipe away her tears and tell her it's all right, and comforted, she will try again.

It's not a big thing to fall down when you're crawling on all fours, because you're already down about as far as you can go.

But one of those sweet days, Samantha will take several steps at a time without falling, and she'll be walking. And it won't be long before walking isn't good enough anymore and she'll learn to run because she wants to get to where she's going in a big hurry.

That's when she'll fall again. This time it will hurt more because she has farther to fall and she'll be going faster and she may bump something on the way down. But again, there'll be someone there to kiss the wounded knee and wash the blood off the scratched elbow and dry the tears, and Samantha will set out again to walk farther and run faster.

The older she grows, the fewer the falls. But when they do come, they'll hurt. Not all her falls will be physical, and those will hurt most of all. That's when she'll need someone to comfort her more than ever.

The time will come in Sammy's life when her steps, however confident and sure, will lead her into falls from which she must recover all by herself. When those of us who are there and watching and aching for her must let her do it by herself, because standing up is ultimately more than just a physical thing.

*Homo sapiens* and Sammy have a lot in common. Through the centuries of our taking those first hesitant steps and learning to walk and run ever faster, we have had our share of falls. At first they weren't that important because they were only small, but the bigger we grew and the faster we ran the more deadly became our "falls." In our "running" we have destroyed peoples, poisoned the earth and developed the means to ensure our own end.

Humanity has now reached the point where if it falls much more there may be no getting up at all. And everyone, it seems to me, is looking for someone to pick us up, tell us we can do better and go try again. No sign of him or her yet.

Hey, it's a long way from a beautiful little girl's first step to the ultimate destiny of the human race. For heaven's sake, to listen to me you'd think the destiny of our race was tied up in the footsteps of a little child.

Whatever way you look at it, you've got to agree on one thing. That first step is a real doozy.

## Through the Looking Glass

They say you can never go back.

But that doesn't stop us from trying. This is the age of reunions and come-homes. Not a cove or a tickle or a school in the province that hasn't had a get-together of some kind this year. The last one I heard about was the Saved-From-Flames Chapter of the Church of the Woolly Haired Sacrificial Lambs, Avalon Division. I'm not a member. Haven't been invited. So I'm not going.

But I've been to several such "dos" this summer. The Brownsdale High School reunion was a chance to meet old friends and make new ones. The fiftieth anniversary of the graduating class of Park Street School in Corner Brook was a memorable affair, mainly because of the energy and enthusiasm of people we normally consider dignified and prim. Springdale itself had a marvellous Come Home time, well organized with lots of activities and a parade that was a credit to all involved.

The Come Home week at Hant's Harbour was the one that I'll remember for a long time.

Hant's Harbour was where I lived and moved and had my being between the ages of ten and fifteen. Adolescence for me was more than just a hair-raising experience. Most of the important "firsts" of my life happened there, and a few I'd just as soon forget.

Being back there again among those with whom I shared those times was a moving and unforgettable experience for me, and I'd like to think they felt the same. At least this time no one beat up on me for being the minister's son.

On the little point of land where I used to sit as a boy and watch the waves roll in and wonder about it all, we had a giant crab leg and caplin roast one night. Can you imagine all the crab and caplin you can eat? And all the milk you can drink? And the magnitude of the headache the next morning?

I got in with bad company on occasion, for which I am thankful, and two days later I'm still not totally recovered. Was it worth it? Does Brian Mulroney have a chin?

It was a great time, as much for whom it was with as for what it was.

Among them, a well-known businessman who long ago gave me my first stamp album and my first record. On one side was "Little Rosewood Casket" and on the other, "Little Buckaroo." The record is long gone, but the words I remember still, along with the kindness of that man for a small boy.

Among them, a lovely lady who taught me how to sing "Beautiful Garden of Prayer" in church, which I did like the little angel I never was.

Among them, a special family with whom I have the kind of relationship that defies the years and the miles, and in whose home I spent much of my time because they treated me as one of their own, which I am and will continue to be.

Look, I have to wax philosophical for the rest of this. You can give it up if you like and go do something else. But this is important to me and I intend to pursue it, so there.

I've been trying to understand what draws us to these reunion affairs, especially those of us well up in middle age. We know perfectly well that those other times we associate with youth and energy and young love don't exist anymore, but still we set out to find them. They tantalize us because they are as close as our strongest memory and as far away as the intervening years. They are so elusive, always lost but never quite gone.

I think in those reunions we try to find the bridge between the reality of the present and the lost world of memory. And we believe that our best bet in finding that bridge is through those whom we knew back then and with whom we can now meet again.

It almost works. OH keeps saying that no woman ever forgets her first love. She says it again and again. It wasn't me. I was the last in a long line. Perhaps he's moved into the neighbourhood or something. Anyway, I hope she's right. Perhaps someone out there is thinking of me that way right now. If so, would you please write and let me know? I need the lift.

Incidentally, it's the same for men, too.

Seeing and being with those who are a special part of your memories has its own magic. They are the only connection, after all, to what once was. Then you find that they are looking to discover their own past in you and that none of you has the key to the magic kingdom. It's a bittersweet truth.

The present is a much more powerful force than the past and when you put the two together, the past just doesn't have a chance. But like the moon affecting the tides and lovers, the past is strong enough to have its own considerable effect. So when you meet those special people from that long ago time, especially after many years have passed, you find yourself not quite in the illusory world of memory and not quite in the reality of the present. Not in the real world we inhabit every day, or the past we try so desperately to find. It's a whole new dimension created by throwing the two together.

It's a different and beautiful and fragile world. And although you don't want your time in it to end, you know in your heart that it must. It's only a world you can visit and not one in which you can live. It's the world of the reunion, when the reunion is at its best.

It's where I was last weekend, and I am grateful.

## Question Period

"May I tell him who's calling?"

Of all the bureaucratic nonsense that inflames my nerves over the run of a week, very little bugs me more than that silly little twit of a question.

I know I'm being unreasonable about this, and if I'm offending you I'm really sorry. You have my approval to write the editor of this esteemed paper and kick some butt, namely mine. Or you can write me personally and upset my family.

Actually, writing to tell me off is really unnecessary because some of my best friends have their secretaries ask this stupid question and can be relied upon to give me a rough time for criticizing it. Others of my friends will criticize the length of that last sentence.

On the other hand, my friends never read this stuff so why should I worry?

The practice, in my view, is extremely bad manners and tends to make people like me somewhat irritated. I am not at my diplomatic best when irritated, especially in the morning.

Secretaries and receptionists are not to be blamed for this, you understand. Someone else is responsible and that someone usually sits in an inside office under a picture of his father or the prime minister and refuses to answer the phone unless he knows it's someone harmless, like me.

I've inquired of those who used to be my friends before this column was printed why they have receptionists ask The Question in the first place. The only reason I've ever heard is that one has to be prepared for whoever's there.

Now I don't know about you, but I haven't had a call from Sadham Hussein in some time, and it's even longer since the Playmate of the Month wanted me. I can see needing time to take a deep breath for Loni Anderson, but apart from that, what in the name of heaven do you have to prepare for? And how much preparing can you do in ten seconds, which is long enough to keep anyone waiting?

What really bothers me is when you answer icily, "Ed Smith," and the person on the other end says sweetly, "One moment, please," and there's this little silence. You know she's on the line to Big Boss and the conversation isn't hard to imagine.

"There's someone named Ed Smith on the phone. Probably not his real name. You wanna take it?"

"Smith? I'm not talking to that idiot. Tell him I'm in a meeting."

You know what it's like? It's like having someone inside call out "Who's there?" when you knock on their door, and then say there's no one home.

To be fair, the reverse feeling is that nice little high you get when the person actually does come on the line after getting your name.

"Gee, she really wanted to talk to me or she would have said she's in a meeting."

It's also sort of nice when the receptionist recognizes your voice without asking. And I don't mind at all when the person answering says, "I'm sorry, she's in a meeting. Would you like to leave your name?"

That gives me a choice, and my ego isn't at risk either way.

Wait a minute! I'm on the wrong side of the argument here. Give me a moment to recoup.

I've worked out several appropriate responses to "May I tell him who's calling?" which someday I mean to use given the right frame of mind. These are for sale and can be purchased by writing to me in care of this paper and enclosing a silent offering.

"No, you may not." That should throw things off for a moment.

If you're calling a man, "Yes, this is legal aid, Paternity Suit Division."

If you're calling a woman, "Just tell her this is the son she never had."

"God." Use a deep voice and you can get the most remarkable silences on the other end.

My own experience is that the more important the person, the less likely it is they'll ask you The Question. I've called cabinet ministers who never know who I am until they're on the line. If a cabinet minister doesn't need to do that, tell me who does. You? Not flipping likely.

Trust someone somewhere to go one better, of course, and the other day I found it. First came The Question, which I answered with stoic calm. But hard on its heels came another, not nearly as bothersome but twice as stupid.

"Is she expecting your call?"

Now how the hell do I know if she's expecting my call? Perhaps someone should go ask her. Perhaps she's been upset for weeks that I haven't phoned, which hardly seems likely since we've never met. Perhaps she isn't expecting my call. Is that of significant importance, given the current world situation? Does she talk only to people she knows in advance are going to call? Should I have called ten minutes ago to let her know my intentions? And above all, what bloody earthly difference could it possibly make?

Perhaps I'm the only one in the province bothered by this stuff. Perhaps it's perfectly legitimate that Important People know who's waiting to talk to them, whether or not they're expected, and why.

I'll be glad to listen to arguments both ways.

May I ask who's reading?

## Those Ferry Blues

You know these little one- and two-day holiday cruises?

The ones on which people like to take jaunts out into the Gulf of Mexico or the Caribbean, usually for a day and a night and a day? It's a kind of status thing for those who don't have the cash or the time to go farther and longer.

Picture it. Safe sunbathing on the hot deck wrapped in a sunblock condom to protect against the UV rays. Swimming naked in a huge hot tub with just you and the Miss America contestants for whom this trip is one of their prizes. Long hot nights in spacious staterooms wrapped in each other's arms for want of something better to do. It's not half bad.

Well, brethren and sistern, OH and I are in the middle of such a little cruise with just a little bit of a twist. We didn't ask for it, we didn't want it and as I write, we're still on it. In the middle of the Gulf of St. Lawrence. For a day and a night and another day and perhaps another night and then possibly another day ...

It isn't hot. We're surrounded by most of the leftover ice from the last two ice ages. The Miss America contestants didn't make it. Neither have OH and I. And we're stuck. It is three o'clock in the morning of the second day. Set 'em up, Joe. Sorry, Ed, the bar is closed.

It began the day before yesterday as most important things do, except love and intestinal gas. The eleven A.M. ferry left around noon of a beautiful spring day. We sang as we drove aboard. Actually, I sang. OH listened and occasionally hummed.

There were eighty-one passengers and two Ed Smiths according to the purser. I thought it a good omen. I was wrong.

Five hours later we were roughly ten miles off North Sydney. Seven hours later we were roughly eleven miles from that same hallowed spot. My good friend Allan and I knew why it was so slow going. We were watching through the windows and realized the captain wasn't picking the best routes through the ice pans. Unfortunately, no one would let us on the bridge to tell him so.

Nine hours later we were in exactly the same place and going nowhere extremely fast. The common term for it is "stuck." It rhymes with another word much in use around the vessel that night.

Finally we are told the bitter truth. The *Caribou* has damaged her rudders. Allan and I nod at each other. The way they were handling the ship it was inevitable. An icebreaker will be along in a couple of hours, they say, to try and get us back to North Sydney. "Stuck" and its sound-alike get even more use.

Sure enough, less than two hours later along comes this dinky (compared with the *Caribou*) little icebreaker and we once again get underway. For a while I watch a full moon playing hide-and-seek with the shadows on the ice. The ice pack has an ethereal, almost otherworldly beauty to it. We don't belong here. We're intruders. I fall off to sleep to the sounds of twelve-foot-thick ice crunching along the sides of the ship. I suddenly awaken to another PA announcement.

The ship has completed turning around, it says, and we are now on our way back to NS. My watch tells me it is three hours since we started moving behind the *Terry Fox*. And we just got turned around?!

I doze off. Again I awaken, this time because there's not a sound in that great, white, wide, wonderful world. I get up and look through the window. Once more we are dead in the ice. The *Fox* is stopped a few hundred yards ahead of us. A steward answers the obvious question.

"Nope, not stuck. Just give up for the night."

Of course.

And then I see it. Two or three hundred yards off to starboard, lights blazing and flags flying, the *Caribou*'s sister ship *Smallwood* is moving freely through the ice pack towards the land I love so well, especially when I can't get to it. I wave, but I don't see anyone wave back.

After daylight and a mug-up, the *Fox* goes back to work and escorts us back to North Sydney. We get in around ten and they drive us off the ship around noon. Twenty-four hours aboard the *Caribou* and we're back to where we started. Stuck.

Later that night, the *Smallwood* returns, takes us all aboard and heads out for parts unknown. At least that's the way her passengers see it. But wonder of wonders, when we wake up this morning there is sunny Port aux Basques in all its glory and we about to enter it.

When we finally get home, our answering machine has this musical message on it from Daughter Number Two. You may sing it to the tune of "She Went into the Water and She Got Her Knees All Wet."

*You were on the ferry when it got stuck in the ice.*
*I know what you were thinking and it wasn't very nice.*
*Be careful of your temper or you're sure to blow a fuse;*
*You've got those ferry blues.*
*You got stuck out on the ferry;*
*I know you were not feeling merry;*
*In fact, I bet you were contrary,*
*You've got those ferry blues.*

Her father's daughter or what!

## Bon Appétit

I spend a lot of time eating in restaurants.

I spend a lot of money eating in restaurants, too, although happily the money isn't always mine. To be more precise, most of it isn't mine, but some of it is. If you've tried to eat three squares a day on the government meal allowance, you'll know you can get gutfoundered in a hurry unless you dig deep into your own pockets for supplementary funding. Eating on the government per diems can be hazardous to your health.

What makes restaurant eating bearable at all is the entertainment factor. This can take several forms, but one of my favourites is watching how people react when they walk through a restaurant door and suddenly find themselves face-to-face with a room full of diners. I've classified them by character type. If you haven't seen them all at one point or another, I'll eat a copy of my next expense claim. The original has to go to the government.

To see these various types at their best, you need to be in one of our more expensive eating establishments. Everybody acts the same at Ponderosa. Ponderosa is the great leveller in diners.

First, there's your Super-Aggressive type. Sports coat, open; loud tie, too short; large stomach; not a lot of hair; jowls. Usually male, but not always. Has just sold his third encyclopedia for the day and wants to celebrate. Doesn't even hesitate as he barrels through the door, knocking over the "Please Wait to be Seated" sign. The room may be full but he's going to have a table, come hell or high water.

His attitude says clearly, "I own this place and everyone in it!" Catch his eye and he thinks you're inviting him to sit with you. You'd rather dine with Saddam Hussein. Waitresses just love this type because he acts as if he owns them, too. For some reason, he's usually alone.

Closely related to the Super-Aggressive is the High and Mighty. High heels, long legs, short dress, trim figure, stylish hair, lots of makeup. Almost always female. Has just come from an executive meeting where she's proven herself superior to men. Carries chin well up off the chest. Upon entering the restaurant, pauses for a moment on the pretense of looking for a table until she's sure everyone's noticed her. Looks to neither left nor right, North nor South.

Her attitude says clearly, "You, especially the males, are well beneath me. I do not notice you. I do not even see you.

"But you may notice me—from a distance."

Once seated, she will produce notes from her briefcase and study them carefully. She is On Her Way Up. If you wish to be noticed by her, it will have to be on her way down. It won't be a long wait.

My favourites for observation purposes are the Husband and Wife. Any husband and wife with more than fifteen years of marital bliss will do. The wife all dressed up to eat out, hair dyed just this side of natural. The husband more casual. They pause to look around the room and decide where to go. Decision made, they head for a table, she in one direction, he the other.

He notices first they've gone their separate ways and briefly struggles with his manly pride before changing course and hurrying after her. Catching up, he makes a half-hearted protest at the embarrassment and then gratefully sinks into a chair at the first empty table. She keeps right on going and sits at the table she had her eye on from the beginning. Beyond embarrassment, he gets up wearily and goes to sit with her. They don't speak.

Trick question. Who carries the money in this family?

The type for whom I have most sympathy is the Hansel and Gretel couple. Middle aged. Plainly dressed. Not well-to-do. Not used to eating out and, like the fairy-tale children, clearly lost. Acutely self-conscious. Obviously thought this was McDonald's. Their attitude is, "Oh Lord, what are we doing in a place like this and how do we get out of it?"

I always feel like rushing up to them and shaking their hands and saying loudly enough for the whole restaurant to hear, "For Pete's sake! Gordon Pinsent! What are you doing here? Loved your last movie! Can I have your autograph? And who's this gorgeous thing with you?"

But I never do. I just let them suffer along until a waitress notices their discomfort and unwittingly traps them into staying, or they get a chance to retreat out the door.

Then there's the Glad-Hander. Almost always male. In politics or sales. Loves to meet people in front of other people. Eagerly scans the diners for a face halfway familiar. Sees one, and rushes over to shake hands and slap shoulders and inquire loudly after relatives he's never heard of. Keeps looking around to see if he's missed anyone. Will keep talking to his current victim until another face from the past is spied. Always knows the waitress by her first name. Always calls the waitress "Ducky" or "Darlin'" or "Dearie"—anything beginning with a *D*. Loves the world and assumes the world loves him. Sometimes it does.

But my favourite type of all is the person who sees you as soon as he enters the door, hurries over and proclaims in a loud voice, "Ed Smith! Boy, I really enjoyed your last book! Everyone should read it!

"And give me that bill!"

## As Old As I Feel

I had a birthday the other day.

Yes, I know. You missed it. So did a lot of other people, not all of them strangers. Would that I could have missed it, too. But these things just keep on coming year after year regular as clockwork.

How old was I? You wouldn't believe me if I told you. Let's just say I'll never see thirty-nine again.

Actually, it turned out to be a great birthday. We were in the Greater Metropolitan Area at the time, and some nice people at the Hospital and Nursing Home Association made me a cake, and we chanced to meet a friend who bought us lunch, and my youngest daughter made me an absolutely delicious dinner, and Other Half ... never mind, but thank you all.

Birthdays aren't as much fun as they used to be. Perhaps it has something to do with age. Groucho Marx once observed that a man is only as old as the woman he feels. OH figured that should hold true for women as well, and was depressed for a week.

My youngest daughter did her best to make me feel better.

"At least, Dad," she said, "you've still got your health."

Isn't that the first thing they say to someone who's just tipped over the hill? "You've still got your health, old and decrepit though you might be. Be thankful for small mercies. Some people your age are in a home. Some people your age are in a graveyard. You can still shuffle along, can you? Great! Still distinguish light from dark at high noon? Wonderful! You've still got your health!" Right.

Youngest daughter isn't easily put off.

"Tell him, Mom," she said to her mother, "tell him he still has that old youthful vitality."

OH regarded me thoughtfully for a long moment. A long, long moment as I lay stretched out on Daughter's chesterfield. I know it's good to think carefully before you speak, and to weigh your words and to consider the implications of what you are about to say. I know all that.

But damn it all, there is a time to just leap right in there, regardless of future shock or effect, and say what needs to be said. OH did.

"I'll have to think about that one from a purely objective perspective," she said carefully, "but he's still young and vital to me."

That's the second thing people say to loved ones who are entering the golden years.

"You're still young to me. You may be older than Methuselah's dog to everyone else, but I can't see any difference in you at all over the last thirty years or so."

All of which is quite true. She's got bifocals and has to stand about five feet from a newspaper to read the headlines. She wouldn't have seen a difference if I'd changed places with Danny DeVito.

The friend who bought us lunch wasn't much help, either, except for buying lunch. He asked how old I was, and I made the mistake of telling him. He patted OH on the shoulder.

"Oh well," he said cheerfully, the way he says everything. "He may not be as good as he once was, but he's probably as good once as he ever was."

Took me awhile to figure that one out and when I did, I wasn't at all sure it was a compliment. OH said he had good intentions, however wrong the comment might have been.

Took me awhile to figure out that one, too.

Someone has said—it wasn't me—that the years a person carries can either weigh him down or bear him up. I know all about the weighing down bit, so I figured it was time to learn something about the bearing up. I picked up a book called *The Men's Health Advisor 1994*. It talked a great deal about how to grow older without growing older, if you follow. Nothing like getting advice from professionals.

One section was advertised as telling you how to have a "bod like a rock." So I read it. Carefully. My conclusion was that the only way for me to have a "bod like a rock" was to die in a desert and become petrified.

One fascinating little health item was that if you knock out a tooth, it will begin to die within fifteen minutes. But if you immediately immerse the tooth in a jar of cold milk, it will stay healthy long enough for you to get to the dentist. Should be really useful if you get a caribou hoof in the teeth up on the Gaff Topsails, or a buoy in the lip hauling lump nets on a long-liner.

Another section in the book was called "Women and Sex" which seemed to make more sense since the two do tend to go together. It turned out to be the shortest chapter in the book. The most interesting fact I found was that polyester underwear can make you impotent.

Still another section talked about "the vast and varied vocabulary of touch as a way to explore the forgotten frontiers of each other's body." Would you have read further? Me neither. I threw the book in the wood furnace and reflected on the forty-odd dollars it cost with a strong feeling of bitterness.

Daughter brought me back to the present.

"Well, Dad," she said seriously, "however old you are, you still have your sanity."

There goes her credibility.

## Art Mirroring Life

This is a "fools rush in" column.

You know. "Fools rush in where angels fear to tread." "Fools rush in where wise men never go," and all that. And where fools rush in columnists aren't far behind. In fact, it's often difficult to tell the difference between them. The truth be known, sometimes there is no difference. This may be one of those times.

Let's talk about the Red Trench.

You've never heard of the Red Trench? Shame on you. The Red Trench is that fascinating piece of sculpture that once graced the walls of Confederation Building, the seat of our provincial government, and now graces the hallowed halls of Memorial University. It lives in infamy because it looks like nothing so much as a ... as a ... well, like a ... you know ... a ...

Delicacy, and a strong feeling for the sensitivities of my readership, is an inhibitive factor here, but let us say that what it looks like for all the world is that portion of the human body peculiar to the female of the species. You may know it as the vagina, Ma'm.

The body is nothing to be ashamed of, to be sure, but most of us do treat that part of our anatomy, male and female, with modesty and respect, unless we've been asked to pose for *Penthouse* or *Playgirl*. That's not a decision I've had to make, but I'm told everyone has a price, including me.

Point is, it's not easy to write about the Red Trench without being vulgar and uncouth. I will do so, of course, but only because I am especially skilled in that area, and can write about practically anything without succumbing to coarse language. Let us carry on.

As a sometime patron of the arts, I have made a noble attempt to study the work from an unbiased viewpoint. As with any piece of art, the primary question is, what is the artist trying to say here? The artist, God rest his soul, didn't have a lot to say about it to my knowledge, other than point out that he hadn't intended it to be a ... a ... you know.

I'm told he smiled a lot when talking about it, but that probably means nothing. He probably smiled a lot when doing it, too.

In my view, having never met him, he was a man with an excellent sense of humour and more than a passing knowledge of the female anatomy. On the other hand, perhaps he was totally ignorant of the female body and had no idea what he was sculpting. Perhaps his hand was guided by an alien presence, or a presence of some other kind. Hard to say.

I searched the piece for some subtle and delicate little ... something that would lift one's mind out of the common physical and sexual basis for observation and into the realm of a more spiritual and aesthetic appreciation. I looked closely, as thousands have before me. Definitely nothing hidden. Practically nothing of a spiritual nature observable. My mind remained firmly rooted in the baser elements.

My conclusion was that the Red Trench is nothing more or less than what it appears to be. I remember wondering at the time what in the name of Masters and Johnson, Kinsey, Freud and Dr. Ruth was this thing doing hanging in Confederation Building, the provincial seat of government?

Was it there as a comfort and/or inspiration for those civil servants who labour night and day for our greater welfare? Was it a symbol of better things to come? Was it a sign of where we are heading? Was it symbolic of a hedonistic philosophy which urges us to eat, drink and be merry for tomorrow we're going to be in even deeper?

Sadly, no one knew.

Then suddenly, the Red Trench disappeared. Just like that it was gone. But where? It didn't turn up in the Louvre or the Smithsonian. Someone suggested it had been bought by the Americans to help with the restoring of the Statue of Liberty at the time. You know, make her as lifelike as possible.

Another group insisted it had been purchased by Memorial's medical school as a manipulative teaching aid. This may have been closest to the mark because where does it turn up now? Exactly. In Memorial's art gallery. You devil, President May!

While student opinion on the question seems to be divided, I have some difficulty with the idea of placing this work in full view of university students. What effect will observing it on a daily basis have on already raging hormones? I ask this in the context of the first-year student from Notre Dame Bay who took one look at the Red Trench and proclaimed loudly, "Sure, I knows she!"

Is it sheer coincidence that shortly after the Red Trench is hung, two students go berserk in the library and begin ripping each other's clothes off? You can understand them going off the deep end in the back seat of a Chevy. But the library?! Boggles the mind. One cannot avoid asking the question of how much one or both of these young people were influenced by that sculpture.

Incidentally, the young man who fled the library leaving his girlfriend nude and alone should in no way be considered a suitable candidate for Student of the Year. In my view, he's right down there with the chap who had the affair with Princess Di and then wrote a book about it. Scummy on both counts.

I have one last thought. My advice would be to remove the Red Trench from MUN's cloistered corridors and place it on a large pedestal at the entrance to Port aux Basques harbour, like the Statue of Liberty on Ellis Island in New York. The symbolism would be obvious.

What federal governments have been doing to us for years.

# To Care or Not to Care

Love is big business.

Especially when you're talking about the world's oldest profession. Those who cater to the whims and needs of hot-blooded and/or lonely males are not on my mind at all today. Indeed, seldom are.

Besides, the government is trying to legislate the ladies of the night off the streets, especially during the winter months when they might catch cold. After all, they don't wear a lot, do they? And if they all get the flu the government will have to support them through Medicare. The governments of the day don't like that very much, which is why they're trying to persuade sex-trade workers to come in out of the cold.

I bet you thought government was acting out of a deep sense of moral concern. Not quite. I'm here to tell you that government's motives are as pure as the driven slush. Always are. Sorry to disappoint you.

Apart from all that, love is big business. Caring is big business. Everyone loves everyone else except for those we know too well. There's a local radio station, for example, which says it cares, and who am I to say they don't? They actually worry about what happens to each and every one of us. They care even if you don't listen to their station, which you must admit calls for one helluva lot of love.

I listen to CBC quite a bit and not once has anyone from that august corporation even suggested she loves me or is the least bit concerned about me. The fact that I'm paying for the whole she-bang with my taxes makes not the least bit of difference. Of course you're paying your share, too, and you can be assured the CBC loves you just as much as it loves me.

If we were subsidizing that other station, Lord knows what would happen in terms of caring. We'd probably have disc jockeys rapping on our doors every night just to make sure we were all home and tucked safely into our beds. The CBC? Hardly. Still, I like to believe that Debbie Cooper cares for me just a smidgen.

The other day I saw a gas station with a big sign out front declaring, "WE CARE." Isn't that nice? However, the sign didn't say what they care about. Is it really about me, the customer? Are they worried I'm not getting enough fibre in my diet? Is some important multi-national oil executive sitting at his desk on the thirty-third floor of his Edmonton office building in a great state of anxiety that I may not be regular? It sort of warms the cockles of my heart, not to mention the cockles in other parts of my anatomy, to think so.

When I go into a gas station I'm not looking for lasting per-sonal relationships or endless love. I'm looking for gas. And I really don't care if they care or not. To be brutally honest, I don't really care that much about them. I know it sounds harsh, but there it is. If they really cared about me they'd lower the price of gas.

I believe Mother Teresa when she says she loves the poor. I believe those of you who write to tell me that God loves me, despite my errant ways. I believe the Queen when she says nothing at all about loving any of us.

I have a little more difficulty believing the fellow with the plunger in one hand and the Sani-Flush in the other when he says he cares about what happens in my toilet bowl. One must separate the wheat from the chaff in those things, you know. Do you really believe the giddy little actress in the awards show who cries to the world, "I love you all!"?

I'm more inclined to believe Hawkeye Pierce of *M\*A\*S\*H* when he said to the nurses, "I may not have loved you all, but I loved as many of you as I could." Would that we all could say that with the same degree of honesty.

Actually, I'm getting pretty cynical about the whole thing. I'm not even sure anymore that Jean Chrétien loves me. I'd settle for Sheila Copps, if that's an option.

Does Bill Clinton care deeply about Monica? Does Stats Canada take the census because they love us? Do we have a moratorium on cod-fishing because the Department of Fisheries and Oceans loves Newfoundlanders? Or fish? Difficult questions all, but fundamentally related to the larger issue of universal caring.

Let's not be too negative about all this. No doubt there are people out there who do care about the rest of us—Conrad Black, Donald Trump. The fact that most of them are trying to sell us something has nothing to do with it.

There I go being cynical again. The truth is that all kinds of nice people do care about us and prove it every day of their lives. I don't mean to make light of that. Why, there are people who read this column simply because they're afraid my feelings will be hurt if they don't. That's not something to make fun of.

My shots at the caring phenomenon are reserved for those who use caring and love as advertising gimmicks, and thus cheapen that most sacred principle of life. For the record, I don't include the local radio station in that lot because they do a great deal of charity work themselves. Just want to be clear.

Caring about others is more than saying it. It involves pain and sacrifice because the act of caring so intertwines our lives around those we love that we can do nothing that does not affect them for better or worse. It's a flawed process that can bring total despair or boundless joy. What does the song say? "The going up is worth the coming down." Perhaps.

So if I said I love you all would you believe it?

Me neither.

## Lessons for Monday

"I am a part of all that I have met."

That was fine for Tennyson's *Ulysses*, but if I'm a part of everything I've met no wonder my father calls me "a queer stick." "Queer," I hasten to point out, is meant in its original sense. Father is of the old school. So, in that regard, am I.

What Ulysses meant was that everywhere he went in his travels and everyone he met had had a profound effect upon him. He may have also meant that he was always learning something from other people. He may have been talking about the girls on the wharves. I prefer to take the more noble interpretation.

Practically every weekend I'm off to some group or other, bringing joy and cheer to select and deserving hearts. Select and deserving because they pay my fee without murmur or complaint, at least to me. I don't care how much they complain to each other.

I don't usually mention those places and events in "The View," despite the fact there's always someone who says jovially and hopefully, "No doubt we'll read all about this in the column next week," which they rarely do and about which I always feel guilty.

There are two reasons to bring up this stuff. The first is to thank all those wise and wonderful people who think I'm worth having over to dinner, which I am, and for always treating me as though I were as important as I sometimes think I am. And the second is to point out that, like Ulysses, I am always learning something at those things and from those people.

Some of what I learn is especially significant for Monday. Next Monday is the day on which Newfoundlanders vote either to bring our denominational schools under one non-denominational roof, or leave things hopelessly divided forever.

Last weekend is a good example. On Friday night, OH and I were with the Knights of Columbus in King's Cove, and on Saturday with the same group in Melrose. Well, it wasn't exactly the same group, but it was the same organization, okay? Knights of Columbus. Lovely crowd in both places.

So what'd I learn? I learned that the loneliest feeling on God's earth is to be a Protestant at a Knights of Columbus dinner when they bless the meal and you're at the head table in full view of the crowd and you don't know how to cross yourself. There's no such thing as a good old Methodist grace with that lot. So I'm never sure what's going to upset God more, that I didn't say grace or that I get all crossed up in the crossing. It doesn't seem to bother OH at all. Very little does.

I learned that lightning does not strike a good Protestant dead if he drinks a toast to the Catholic Church, which I did and it didn't, so there. I also drank to the Knights of Columbus, although I did note in passing there was no toast to the Orangemen. Perhaps they didn't know that I was once an Orangeman. Perhaps they didn't give a fig newton.

I did not raise my glass insincerely in those toasts, I assure you, since I have great respect for all involved. But I should point out that when I'm in imminent danger of having to make a speech, I'll drink to anything. Or nothing.

I have always maintained that Protestants in general can learn a lot from Catholics. Catholics do not allow their speakers to pay for their drinks. If Protestants could learn just that one lesson, it would suffice for this decade.

In Melrose I learned a whole new philosophy of life from the worthy knight who was MC. Not only does he claim to have read everything I've ever written—obviously an intelligent fellow with excellent taste—but also he gave me this great creed to live by as we were digging into the cold plate.

Remember the "one important thing" that Billy Crystal learned in *City Slickers*? Well, it wasn't that. If you haven't seen that film, by the way, you should. It's not only very funny, but it can teach us a lot about ourselves. You'd also have the advantage of knowing what I was just talking about.

Where was I? Oh yes, a creed to live by. Get ready to cut this one out and stick it to your fridge door.

"Always have a good excuse."

That's it. Like all great pronouncements, it's as simple as it is profound. Consider how many fewer nights you would have spent on the living room sofa had you been living by that commandment, and at least one other. Think of where you'd be in your profession today if you had had the right excuse when it mattered most. Think of how much better your chances will be of avoiding eternal damnation by adhering to that creed.

I tell you, brethren and sistern, the long road of life is littered with the spiritual, marital, and professional corpses of those who could not come up with the good excuse at the propitious moment.

I'll tell you something else. Some of life's greatest lessons are learned over the beet salad.

The real things I learned from the good people of King's Cove and Melrose and others like them? I learned that we can be different without being divided; that we can share in the richness of each other's traditions and heritages without diminishing our own; that instead of tearing us apart, those differences can actually bind us closer together; and that, in the final analyses, we are judged by history, and perhaps by God, for the degree to which we come together as a people.

I'll just have to learn to cross myself properly.

## Election Premises

*Good morning, Big Ed. Do you have a few moments for the media?*

I always have a few moments for the media. I might say, though, that the media have precious few moments for me. Is there a reason for that?

*We're not sure. At this time, we believe the public is anxiously awaiting your views on the upcoming federal election and would like to ask you a few questions. Okay?*

I live and breathe for nothing else.

*Good. First, what party do you currently support?*

Neither. Supporting a political party in the middle of an election is an immoral act.

*You mean you support the candidate rather than the party?*

Supporting the candidate is an even greater immorality. I have nothing to do with either.

*Okay, what about the issues, then? What issues and concerns do you see needing to be dealt with in this campaign?*

None. The Soup Girl said last week that—

*Just a minute, Big Ed. The "Soup Girl"?*

Yes, Kim Campbell. She said there were some issues that should never be discussed in an election. She was right, too, as far as she went. My view is that the only issue worth talking about between now and October twenty-fourth is whether or not coloured toilet paper is bad for your health.

*Gee, Big Ed, you do have a unique perspective on things. But if you don't support parties or candidates, and if you don't discuss the issues in the election, what's the point of having an election at all?*

You are betraying an abysmal ignorance over the real purpose of the federal election. This has nothing to do with parties or candidates or issues.

*No? What does it have to do with?*

Egos.

*Fascinating. Could you explain further?*

I could and, happily for you, I will. Winning an election, any election, is one awesome power trip. You throw yourself into the dirtiest and deadliest game of them all with no quarter asked and none given, and when you come out on top you think you're God, which is why so many politicians have trouble remembering that they're not.

*I see. But don't you think—*

I'm not finished. It takes a nice slice of ego to present yourself to the country as the one and only person in the whole shebang who can resolve all our problems and wipe away all tears from our eyes. It takes a fair bit to believe it yourself.

*Very interesting!*

Isn't it, though? Who do you think cares about parties or issues, other than as a means to getting elected? Haven't you noticed how each party leader is careful to say only those things that are deemed to be acceptable to the majority of people? Tell me, what's the first duty of any politician?

*To serve the people.*

You betray a stark ignorance of the facts. The first duty of any politician is to get elected, by whatever means necessary. There's no issue as important as that. And that in itself doesn't mean politicians are bad people. But do you really believe that any person running for any seat in the country is saying what he or she actually thinks about anything these days?

*Well, I—*

Be quiet and listen to your betters. Politicians running for office say only what they think you, the voter, want to hear, and that's fair enough. How else are they to get elected? I once heard a clergyman tell his congregation what he really thought about God and heaven and hell and all that, and it was damned interesting stuff, too.

*What's your point, Big Ed?*

It wasn't what the congregation wanted to hear. So they fired him and hired someone who told them only what they themselves believed. Wasn't much point in discussing anything important with that fellow, though.

*So?*

You weren't breast-fed, were you? What's the point of discussing issues and concerns with any candidate in any party when you know that the candidates will say only what they think people want to hear? How can you decide which party or candidate to support when you know that at the moment their whole being is geared to getting themselves elected? That was your question, was it not?

*Yes, I guess so. So you aren't going to vote?*

Of course I'll vote. That's the sacred duty of every citizen in a democracy. Where on earth did you get that idea?

*I don't know. But if you vote, how will you decide for whom to vote?*

Simple. I always vote for the underdog.

*How do you know which one is the underdog?*

The underdog is always the last one on the ballot.

*But they're listed alphabetically and I fail to see—*

Does your mother know you're out? Ever know anyone anywhere whose name began with a Z to get elected to anything?

*Gee whiz, Big Ed, thanks a lot for this. It's obvious why you yourself have never sought public office.*

That's right. No one's asked me.

## Schools Gone to Hell

*In 1994 government made a concerted effort to do away with the old denominational school system in Newfoundland and Labrador and replace it with a public school system. The United and Anglican Churches together with the Salvation Army had integrated their schools many years before. The issue was bitterly contested.*

I don't know what's wrong with you crowd.

According to recent surveys conducted by such responsible and reliable groups as the government, most of you want to toss the current denominational school system out the stained-glass window. Shame on you. Tsk tsk tsk.

I put this unhealthy attitude down to being totally out of touch with currently modern standards in education, religion and moral values. I wish to speak to all three at this time. No doubt you wish to listen. That makes us compatible, although probably not for long.

In case you're wondering, I am an expert. I went to school. This seems to be the major criterion for any and all expertise in the issue. It doesn't matter how long a person attended. Anyone who went to school at all is automatically an expert on education. You don't believe me, tune in to *Open Line* or read the letters section of this dear paper.

Moreover, on occasion I go to church which, to follow the same reasoning, makes me an expert on churches as well as denominational education. Best of all I went to United Church schools in outport Newfoundland and this makes me an expert on everything from scribblers to the button-up fly.

So let's talk about education and the truth as I see it.

It's been said that the denominational school system produces students who are beneath their Canadian counterparts in virtually any subject area you care to mention. But that simply isn't true. I'd match the students in our Newfoundland schools against any school in Toronto, Edmonton or Vancouver on such topics as The Rapture, the Second Coming or the Papal View of Contraception.

On second thought, I think I'd leave Integrated Schools students out of it.

I'd put money on the students in our "Christian" schools in a debate with any secondary centre of learning in the country on the question of whether one is saved by good works or grace alone. As an aside, let me point out that given the high level of unemployment and the even higher level of illiteracy in

Newfoundland, grace as a means to salvation is growing in popularity because good work of any kind is so scarce.

Let's face it, there are those heathen souls who would dismiss religion as a valid measure of the worth of denominational schools, so let's examine the bigger picture. The statistics are out and there can be no doubt about it. In general tests of basic skills, students at all grade levels in Newfoundland schools are almost as good as the national average. Only a few percentage points separate them overall from children anywhere else in Canada.

So what else in the name of heaven do we want? For our children to be almost as good as youngsters Upalong is the dream of every Newfoundland parent, is it not? Generations of Newfoundlanders before us have strived to be almost as good as mainlanders. It's been our *cause célèbre*, our raison d'être and, just in case you're sick of French, our Holy Grail. Now that we almost have it, there are those who would take it away from us!

"Shame!" I cry, and again "Shame!"

There's just one other area to consider: values and morals. We want to keep the church presence in our classrooms because without it children have no chance of ever learning either.

This has been amply demonstrated on the mainland. Consider the barbaric and totally unchristian lifestyle of the Annapolis Valley, for example. One has only to drive through that hedonistic culture in early autumn to see the naked symbolism associated with the fall of man and, not far behind him, woman. See the trees loaded with apples, the very stuff of sin, and men and women no doubt urged on by each other plucking fruit in the most carnal fashion. It's enough to give one the spiritual dry heaves.

In hundreds of thousands of homes across this land, children condemned to learning in non-denominational schools are growing into adults totally bereft of such values as honesty, integrity, compassion and charity. Lust and greed rule supreme and the combined weight of both home and creed are powerless against a rapacious and morally void public school system.

"Enough!" I hear you cry loudly. "Enough! Never thought I'd see Smith so sarcastic, so negative!"

Really? You're surprised? Smith, who proudly spent almost thirty years of his teaching life in the Integrated School System where the churches concerned have put the education of their children ahead of the perpetuating of their individual confessional stances?

Smith, whose clergyman father together with his colleagues in other denominations, spent countless hours and endless energy trying to bring the different denominations together into amalgamated systems long before the era of integration?

Smith, who had his humble beginnings in St. Anthony where one of the great Christians of our time, Sir. Wilfred Grenfell, condemned denominational schools as a curse upon the land?

Yes, Smith. And the only regret I have in stating my view is the possibility of losing some of my friends in those other systems. I hope friendship doesn't depend on shared opinion.

Some years ago as an English teacher in one of those progressive, amalgamated schools I found this sentence in an essay written by a Grade Nine student. The truth and the insight have been with me ever since.

"There are five different denominations in this town," he wrote, "but it can only be noticed on Sundays."

Out of the mouths of babes.

# The Devil Didn't Make Them Do It

Jack the Ripper. The Boston Strangler. Gary Gilmore.

Names to strike terror into the very bowels. They committed the most unspeakable acts of horror against their victims, and caused untold suffering and grief. And they are only three of a long line of serial killers and psychopaths who, along with door-to-door religion peddlers, have plagued society for generations.

Turns out they weren't such bad fellows after all. Apart from a small chemical imbalance, or a piece missing in the frontal lobe of the brain, these were ordinary chaps much the same as you and me. The terrible things they did were caused by a physical abnormality and not the basic evil in their souls or a lack of fibre in their diet.

Such is a new theory being advanced by researchers who claim that knowing the difference between good and evil, or even caring about it, is not a spiritual thing at all. It's all the result of a physical abnormality, like an ingrown toenail.

Scientists have discovered that part of the brain which they say is responsible for value development and moral judgments. In most of us, it develops normally and we turn out fine. In some people, it is either poorly developed or missing altogether and the result is a Son of Sam or a Charlie Manson or a televangelist— people incapable of assessing situations on an ethical basis or distinguishing between right and wrong.

An essay in *TIME* stated that, in an effort to shed more light on this idea, scientists are studying the battered skull of one John Gage. Mr. Gage, who lived many years ago, was playing with dynamite one day when it exploded prematurely and drove a steel bolt the thickness of a broom handle in through his left eye and out the top of his head.

One would have expected Mrs. Gage to immediately adopt the honorary titles of "widow" and "beneficiary," but amazingly Gage didn't even pass out. He lived for years after, his mind and faculties unimpaired except for a rather large hole in his head and a missing eye. Nothing too serious.

There was, however, one little problem. Previous to his accident, Gage had been a reliable, sober and God-fearing person. Immediately after, he became such a disgusting reprobate that he couldn't hold a job and people refused to be in his company. Aha, the boys reasoned, the part of the brain that told him to be good was destroyed by the steel bolt.

The theory does not allow for the possibility of Mr. Gage being so peed off at the world that he simply said the hell with it.

So there you have it. If you don't love your mother it's because a piece of your brain is missing. If you hate your neighbour, you could have a chemical imbalance. If you rob and rape and murder indiscriminately, something inside your skull didn't develop the way it was supposed to. If you're Saddam Hussein, the only one who can explain you is George W. Bush.

The implications of this new theory are staggering.

Think what it does to the churches. Here they've been preaching for centuries that it's the devil who makes people do bad things, and all we need to be good is a healthy dose of whatever brand name religion is currently on the go.

Now we're told Oral Roberts and Billy Graham have nothing to do with it. Religion has nothing to do with it. The devil has nothing to do with it.

The problem is with a discreet little area of the brain which in some individuals doesn't develop as it should. So what will happen to sermons and the experience of Being Saved? What about going out and bringing them in from the Fields of Sin? Where does this leave the concept of Original Sin and Redemption? The effect on collection plates could be devastating.

And think of the poor devil himself or herself. He's been taking credit for the presence of evil amongst us for so long that he was beginning to believe it. The televangelists blame him or her for everything from cheating on income taxes to murder most foul. Now we find the devil is an imposter, taking credit under false pretenses and having no more power than a Liberal back-bencher.

Sad, in a way, to see someone fall from such heights to such depths, not to mention what it does to what's left of the credibility of televangelists.

Imagine being able to isolate that part of the brain responsible for knowing right from wrong and fixing it so it works as it should from birth. No more war, no more crime, no more federal fisheries scientists.

And what about punishment for serial rapists and killers? Should we be sending them to the brain surgeon rather than the electric chair? Would it be possible to identify the problem in infants and repair the damage immediately?

Think what a world we would have! The government would have to come up with a retirement package for prison guards, psychiatrists and ministers of the gospel. We wouldn't need them anymore. Lawyers would become extinct and little old ladies could walk the streets at night in peace, as could little young ladies if there was any call for it.

The future is only a heartbeat away, and beckoning us onward. Thanks to genetic engineering, children will not only be superintelligent but also born free of the genes that cause diseases. Their sense of values will be as highly developed as their moral judgment and they will see no evil, hear no evil and do no evil. No more gambling, no more adultery, no more lewd thoughts about the opposite sex ...

Does it strike you that the world is going to be one hell of a dull place?

## Slaughter of the Innocent

I have this friend.

Actually, she's more than a friend but we don't want to get into the details of personal relationships here. Let's just say we're close and leave it at that. And we'll call her Pat because Pat is my sister's name and she wouldn't mind me using it for illustrative purposes. Allow me, too, to assure the gentle reader that this account is the gospel truth. You have my word on it.

Pat is just the tiniest bit naive. She's the type who's always being sent to find a left-handed monkey wrench or a size twelve skyhook. She's a bright little soul, mind you, but she has this tendency to believe everything she's told and to trust people who shouldn't be trusted.

Enter Cousin Al. We do have to give these people identities and Pat and Al are as good as I can come up with at short notice.

Cousin Al is a devil. The devil twinkles in his eye and gleams in his grin. Each ear has its own resident imp acting in an advisory capacity. His main aim in life is to take advantage of people like Pat. Every family has a Cousin Al. Which wouldn't be a problem if every family didn't also have a Pat. But, of course, every family does. Enter problem.

Pat's husband, whom we'll call Poor Willie, again for identification purposes, developed a bad case of athlete's foot. Which again wouldn't have been so bad if he'd had anything else athletic to go along with it. But since Poor Willie is to athlete what O.J. Simpson is to innocence, the thing became a nuisance that wouldn't go away. Those of us who have had athlete's foot and/or jock itch can relate.

Anyway, Poor Willie tried everything he could over a period of several weeks to clear up the condition. Nothing worked. His foot got worse and worse. Finally, he took to soaking it in water and baking soda each night because that at least gave him some temporary relief. It was on such a night that Cousin Al and his girlfriend walked in and Pat's fate was sealed.

Cousin Al showed great interest in Poor Willie's condition. He even indicated some concern and asked detailed questions about what remedies had been tried and what advice had been taken and from whom.

Finally, he drew Pat out into the kitchen and spoke to her in a low whisper.

"I think we have a real problem here," he said, "and if we don't arrest it now, Willie could wind up losing his foot."

Pat was flabbergasted, and not a little alarmed.

"You don't mean it, Al!"

"Oh yes," said Cousin Al. "I've seen this sort of thing before. Leave it untreated for any length of time and it's game over."

"Oh my," whispered Pat in a panic, "he's had this for weeks."

"Exactly," said Al. "We don't have much time to lose."

"What's he got, anyway?" Pat was on the verge of tears.

There was the tiniest of pauses before Al answered.

"Hoof and mouth disease. But for God's sake don't say anything about it to Willie because he'll get all upset and stress will just speed up the disease."

"But what can I do, Al? Should we call an ambulance?"

"No," whispered Al. "I was reading just the other day about a new product that's just been approved for hoof and mouth disease. I'm not sure that it's reached St. John's yet, but we could try. Are the drugstores still open?"

"There's one about a half hour away from here that might be. I'll phone and see if they have it."

Hope raised her beautiful head as Pat ran for the phone. The line was busy.

"That means they're still in," said Al. "Best you get over there fast. Remember to ask for Hoof and Mouth Cream."

Pat was gone like a shot.

To her tremendous relief, the drugstore was still open. Through the door she flew and headed straight for the drug counter.

"I need some Hoof and Mouth Cream," she said breathlessly, "and I need it now. Please don't say you don't have any."

"But of course we have treatments for Hoof and Mouth," replied the druggist. "But I need to know how old he is."

"He's forty-seven."

"Forty-seven?" The druggist raised his eyebrows. "That's very old. How long has he been troubled with this?"

"Several weeks," replied Pat, almost in tears again. "I know we let it go for too long but I didn't understand ..."

"That's okay," said the druggist kindly. "Just where is your horse now?"

"My what?"

"Your horse."

"But I don't have a horse."

"If you don't have a horse, Ma'am, who has the hoof and mouth problem?"

"My husband!"

There was a moment's silence. The druggist coughed. Then he coughed again. Suddenly a violent spasm shook his entire body and he turned away bent over double. Finally he straightened up and, with tears running down his face, said chokingly, "Lady, you've been had."

Cousin Al left for the mainland shortly after this affair and no one has seen much of him since. I'm told he returns for brief visits.

Poor Willie never complained of athlete's foot again.

## Just Keep on Truckin'

I have this old truck.

She's been kicked around a bit in the eleven years we've been together. The major dent along the side was put there by me scant days after I bought it. I was showing an admiring family and a skeptical OH how a 4x4 could go over old logs and stumps and rocks and boulders. She went, but not without some personal sacrifice.

That first week was a rough one for my new, shiny black pickup. I came home one day to find Number One Son, then about eight years old, busily cleaning the snow off the hood with a steel rake. The gouges are still there.

One of the doors was partially ripped off by that same Son some nine years later when he was backing up while looking ahead. It was partially repaired courtesy of a hammer, and opens with great screeching protests. The other door opens to a magical combination of lifts and twists known only to me.

Every once in awhile someone will call to see if I'm interested in selling my little pickup. They always hang up before I stop laughing.

A friend who is among those unfortunates who have to pass by my truck in order to get into and out of our place of business recently remarked that much of my recent history could be read from the pan of my truck. He was too polite to actually say so, but it was obvious he considered that history to be less than savoury.

It struck me that he was right. That the pans of pickup trucks are like the tops of office desks. A great deal can be said about the owners from their current and habitual states. I began to consider what my truck had to say about me.

I have hauled and do continue to haul in that truck, among other things: kelp, sawdust, wood, horse manure, cow manure, assorted and unassorted garbage, various species of fish, various types and quantities of soil and sundry other items associated with the life of your average outport person. Each of these varying commodities tends to leave some small part of itself behind in the pan long after the bulk of the original material has been taken out.

There are also those things that I mean to take down to the cabin on the very next trip, and those things brought up from the cabin several trips ago to be returned to the house. There are those things destined to be taken down aboard the boat at first opportunity and those things taken out of the boat to be brought back up here at precisely the same time.

There are also those things which I cannot throw away because I am a pack rat, but which as yet have found no permanent home. A quick check of my truck this afternoon shows that this includes at the moment, and in addition to the aforementioned leftovers: some pieces of carpet, some containers of motor oil, a piece of Plexiglas, a couple of cans of paint, a wooden buoy, a short length of tailpipe, assorted lengths of rope, a case of empties and a can of gas for the chainsaw which will shortly double as a can of gas for the snowmobile. The snowmobile is older than the truck and in even worse shape, so the gas may be superfluous this season.

For some reason OH refuses to drive the truck except in cases of extreme emergency, such as having no other way to get to her card club.

You may wonder why I'm telling you all this. I am wondering why you're still reading. I'll try to explain the first. I doubt if anyone can explain the second.

Since the time of my friend's remark, I have begun to sneak looks into the pans of other people's trucks and what I find is most discouraging. You could virtually eat out of those other pans. Of course, you could eat out of mine, too, if you weren't fussy about what you ate and didn't mind sharing with others of God's creatures.

The thing is, other people's trucks are invariably cleaner than the proverbial whistle. And what does this tell us? Simply that these are the kind of people who never have anything interesting in their trucks. Their trucks lead boring lives. I suspect that they do, too. Have a good look around the trucks with the clean pans and try to find a dent with a story in it. The trucks, like the lives of the owners, are mainly for show. Nothing substantial or interesting ever happens in either. At least that's my hypothesis.

An alternative theory is that these owners put plastic in the backs of their trucks when they're hauling guck, and clean and sweep them out on a regular basis. No matter what was in the pan yesterday, therefore, today everything is bare and clean. Perhaps that's what happens. But I don't know how they manage it. On the rare occasions I try to give my truck a good cleaning, I never seem to work long enough to get all the dirt and garbage totally out of it.

The pans of our trucks are a bit like life, you know, when you stop and think about it. If you have to ask me how you aren't paying attention.

Anyway, my old truck and I have a lot in common. We're both still on the road bearing the scars and carrying the leftovers of other times. I don't know which one of us will succumb first, but appearances to the contrary, one thing is certain.

Neither of us will rust out.


## In Deeds Not Years


My friend Wilfred passed away last week.

In his dying he taught everyone who knew him in these last few months everything there is to know about living. I'd like to tell you about him.

Wilfred discovered he had cancer partway through his course in Motor Vehicle Repair at our campus two short years ago. He was a promising student with a natural ability in mechanics and to see him have to give up the program was nothing short of tragic. But even throughout the ordeal of his treatments he kept promising that he'd be back.

And he was. Last fall he took on the task of shop support worker for other students, and worked so diligently that at the spring graduation he was awarded his MVR certificate.

But the cancer was spreading, and in September we learned that the prognosis was not good. He was taken to St. John's for further treatment, but last week he decided that further effort was futile and returned to Springdale where he died a couple of days later.

Wilfred was twenty-two years old.

One would think that Wilfred hadn't lived long enough to acquire the wisdom we associate with age, or the courage and patience that comes from facing all the "natural heartaches that flesh is heir to" in its normal season of living. His life wasn't long enough to have the fullness of marriage and children and growing old, and the acceptance of inevitable death that comes with it. In fact, Wilfred wasn't old enough to die at all, especially in the full knowledge of that reality.

I have watched many people die. But neither I nor anyone else has ever seen anyone of any age die with more courage, more patience and more acceptance than Wilfred showed on his deathbed last week.

Several of us from the campus went to see him that last day. He had been told the night before that his remaining time was to be measured in hours. He was propped up in bed and he was smiling. The old gentle sense of humour that we loved so much about him was still there, and it was obvious that he was doing his best to put his visitors and his family as much at ease as possible. He talked to his instructor about how much the campus was like a family and how much he loved it there. And he talked to me about moose hunting.

It was Father and Wilfred who got our moose last year. On a rainy, squally evening when I was out of town, Wilfred volunteered to guide Father through the country he knew and loved. And lo and behold, with Wilfred's sharp eyes and Father's deadly aim, down came a fine young bull.

Father never got over the kind of people Wilfred and his family at Sheppardville were. Several men went back into the woods with them after dark that night and took care of everything. They paunched and cleaned the animal, brought it out to the woods road and hung it in their shed.

"Those people from Sheppardville," Father kept saying, "are a special breed."

"I didn't get a shot at a moose this year," Wilfred said to me with the twinkle in his eyes not quite masking the pain of speaking, "but in August I did knock down a target for practice."

That was his demeanour for the whole day as, one by one, he spoke to his family and said goodbye to them. As his body grew weaker it seemed his fortitude grew stronger until at last he slipped gently into sleep in the arms of his twin brother and did not awaken.

All of us who knew him had the same thought. We would not be nearly so afraid of dying if we could face it with even half the courage of Wilfred Sheppard. And if he could face dying with that attitude, surely the rest of us can face living the same way. If we could live our lives with the same degree of patience and caring that Wilfred showed in his dying, life would be a great deal richer for everyone.

At the funeral itself, there were no hysterics. Family and friends cried and hugged each other and then tried to smile. And I thought that perhaps the same kind of courage that lets people live that way is what also allows them to die that way.

I came away from Wilfred's funeral inspired, and for a number of reasons. On Monday of last week Sheppardville had no cemetery, not having needed one before. On Tuesday afternoon the little town had a full-sized cemetery fenced and painted and completely cleared. Everyone took the day off from regular jobs and went to work on something they considered far more important. It's what the word "community" used to mean in every Newfoundland town and outport.

Wilfred's ultimate gift was in showing us how to live with dignity and humour, even in the face of imminent death, and that it is not only desirable that we do so, but entirely possible as well.

So the next time I begin complaining about anything, I'll think of Wilfred and how he died, uncomplaining to the end. When I resent what others have that I do not, I'll remember Wilfred and his quiet acceptance of having life taken from him before it had really begun. And if anything ever makes me tend to be bitter toward life or anyone in it, I fervently hope I remember Wilfred and the sweetness of his last hours.

Wilfred came to our campus to learn from us. But for the rest of our lives we will remember him for what he, the student and the boy, taught us who were his teachers and his friends.

Thank you, Wilfred, and goodbye.

## Laughing on the Outside

Time for reflection.

If you're looking for the usual fare of spicy and sparkling wit, it ain't here this week. Sorry. Go read Hansard. I'm in the thoughtful and contemplative mode. For those of you who think they know me, that in itself might be funny enough.

This is the soberest week in the Christian year for most of you. It's hardly the time for frivolity and merrymaking, and even an insensitive soul such as myself gets to thinking a little about the verities of life. I don't actually know what a verity is, but it doesn't sound like a lot of fun.

Most weeks I work fairly hard at trying to bring a chuckle to your dry and sunless lives. I mean, you read the front pages and listen to the newscasts, and all you read and hear is gloom and doom and politics. The pious have their faiths shattered with the betrayals of their leaders, and innocents throughout the world are nailed to other trees.

Reading the pages of your average newspaper hardly makes you want to get up and dance.

That's why I write this column, you know—to give people a momentary chuckle or two at the end of a long week of trials and adversities in the world at large. You don't think it's for the money, do you? Send me a self-addressed, stamped envelope and I'll tell you what a miserable pittance this lot pays me. In fact, I'll tell you anything you want to know. My fan mail has gone from a crawl to a slow trickle lately, and I'm trying to drum up support. I've even thought of writing to myself. But anyway, my dear, this stuff is written especially for you.

Actually, it's not the troubles of the world that really get me down. Trouble is all one can expect in places like Afghanistan and Beirut, given all the heathens over there and everything. Wars and rumours of wars are all they know.

You've got to expect, too, that in a place the size of Earth you'll have your scattered typhoon and earthquake. This is not to be callow or uncaring about these things. It's a matter of inevitability. But these tragedies get lots of attention from just about the whole world, and we support the unfortunates involved as much as possible.

Where I get all hung up is with people like you. Ordinary people with whole backloads of crosses that in some cases no one else knows anything about. Not too many of you reading this who haven't gone through your own private little crucifixion of soul and mind. Some of you, I know, are at your Golgotha even now.

And yet you smile when someone smiles at you, and you laugh at the foolishness that people like me get on with, and to the rest of us you appear serene and undisturbed. No outward sign at all that inside you are shrivelling and dying and unable to reach out, even though you're so afraid. And because the rest of us don't know, we don't offer you any support and leave you to carry on the struggle on your own.

But there's a message for you in this season and at this time, if you want to hear it.

There's almost always someone who cares and who wants to help you carry that load and who will be there for you. You don't have to be alone.

If all else fails you can even write me, but there's got to be someone better around.

In a spiritual sense that's the message of Easter, too, but I'm not into sermons, although this is getting perilously close. Next thing, you'll be sending me silent collections and I can't afford entry into the next income-tax bracket.

You have to forgive the scattered flippancy here. It's not that I'm not serious about this stuff, but some of my readers get all upset when I show any signs of being sober at all. The levity is to keep them happy. This week the heavy part is to keep me happy. Are we all happy now? Good.

I guess I'm like most of you—trying hard not to think too much about the troubles of the world, and concentrating as much as possible on the lighter side. Perhaps I do that a little more than most, but that's my nature and besides, I get paid to write what I'm thinking about. I don't write everything I think, of course. I'd get paid a lot more if I did. And have a lot more readers.

People often ask if I ever have difficulty finding suitable topics for the column. Next to "Do they really pay you for that?" it's the most frequent question I get. And no, it's not normally any trouble at all, as long as I can drag my mind from the tears of the world outside.

But sometimes, when the world for me is not all sweetness and light, and I don't feel very much like laughing myself, I have to reach down pretty deep to be my usual effervescent and vivacious self.

You know how it is with us humourists.

Laughing on the outside, and all that.

## Giving in to Pressure

My blood pressure has always been perfectly normal.

It is important you know this at the beginning. For all my adult life, blood pressure has never been a problem. I'd repeat that if I had time.

Indeed, my doctor told me not long ago that I had the blood pressure of a teenager. Sudden thoughts, unbidden and forbidden, flashed through my mind, and he, reading my mind as a good doctor should, hastened to add, "But don't go running around acting like a teenager."

Manure.

Then a couple of weeks ago I made a terrible mistake.

Other Half and I were in the Annapolis Valley visiting her sister. I had just retired, you see, and life was pleasant and stress-free. The last day we were there, they decided to go on a shopping expedition and invited me along as chauffeur. No problem, I thought to myself. I mean, the Annapolis Valley is probably better known for its apples than its shopping malls. Surfing the New Minas business district isn't exactly the same as plunging into the bowels of the West Edmonton Mall.

Myself must have been asleep at the time. But that wasn't my mistake.

We began the excursion by returning to the house somewhere between four and five times. Each time, we drove a little farther down the road before one or the other discovered something missing, like makeup, purses, stuff to be returned from the last purchasing safari, a sandwich. The last meant to mollify me.

But I smiled benignly throughout until we were finally far enough down Highway 101 that I knew we wouldn't go back for anything, including, as it turned out, me. I'd forgotten my wallet.

Not only did this occasion some comment from the sisters, but also it placed me entirely in their control. Anything I wanted to do on my own while they were shopping, like finding a lunch counter, would first have to be approved by them in the form of a loan or a handout. I became conscious of a certain loss of benignity in my smile, but this still wasn't my mistake.

The first place we went into was a bisexual clothing store. I needed to buy a belt, so I entered with a will. I even "shopped" for it properly, which is to say I followed the example of the women and fingered a few labels and turned over a few items and critically examined belts I wouldn't have bought to hold up someone else's pants. I finally purchased a fine belt of genuine leather and thought I'd done okay since it did a passable job of holding up mine.

OH, however, offered the view that the belt should be holding up three pairs of pants because I paid three times more for it than necessary. She was supported by her sister, repeatedly and at length. At that point I became conscious of losing a considerable amount of the joy of purchase. But that wasn't my mistake, either.

OH's sister had told her son at Acadia that we would meet him at his apartment at three. He had classes immediately before and after so the timing was critical. The drive to Wolfville from New Minas is about ten minutes, so precisely at ten minutes to three, Sister proclaimed we had to get on the road immediately.

I started off for the store entrance at a good clip, looked around and there was Sister heading off at the same clip in the opposite direction.

"Where are you going?" I called.

"There's a 'going out of business' sale down here," she called back.

"But you said we have to leave immediately!" I protested.

"We do," she shouted firmly and was lost to sight.

OH, who had observed all this calmly, couldn't understand my frustration.

"But she said we had to leave immediately and then she did the exact opposite even while saying it!"

"The trouble with you men," said OH, heading for a row of dresses, "is that you can't do two things at the same time. There's no problem here. We'll make it."

We did, but only by the skin of someone else's teeth.

Later, as we prepared to turn out into a busy four lanes of traffic, Sister said, "Turn right here." So I did, turning into the lane which was going my way.

A split second later she shouted, "Oh look! There's a sale up the road there. Turn left! Turn left!" So I did, by this time being on DRD—Direct Response Drive. I careened madly across the other two lanes, leaving part of the paint job on the bumper of a transport truck and the rest on an Annapolis Valley ambulance that was going somewhere in a big hurry, come hell, high water or us. Could that driver swear! But even that wasn't my mistake.

That's how it went for the day.

"Turn right here" would come the command. And I'd swing madly into someone's driveway.

"Not right here!" would come the indignant protest. "I meant the next right."

I had more rigid digits lifted in my direction on that one day than in the whole of my previous long life. By the time we paused at a drug counter on the way home that night, I was ready for the couch and I don't mean daybed.

The drugstore had one of those free blood pressure machines for public use, and OH suggested we should all get a reading. I stuck my arm in the damn thing and that was my big mistake. It read 152 over 102, which evidently is not good.

I protested the machine was wrong. It wasn't. I said it was a one-time reading. It wasn't. Sister, who's a nurse, took it roughly twenty-seven times over the next day. It stayed the same. OH made me go to the doctor and he took the salt out of my diet and threatened to take the lead out of my pencil if I have to go on medication.

I believe I said earlier that I'd always had excellent blood pressure.

Right up until retirement.

# The Season of Our Discontent

For sheer absolute stupidity, nothing beats it.

It's an exercise more useless than trying to talk sense in the House of Assembly. It would be less a waste of one's time to attempt to bring decorum to the St. John's Municipal Council. It would be more productive to set up a Welcome Wagon branch in Iraq. Your time would be better spent endeavouring to establish a chapter of the Bible Society in the Playboy mansion.

I'm talking about sowing vegetable seeds in Newfoundland.

Every "spring" we do it. Every cold, wet and miserable June, Other Half and I put on our long underwear, get into our raingear, pull on our long rubbers, haul on our mitts and venture out into the garden. We try to sink spades into semi-frozen earth. We wrestle with rocks and sticks, and the roots from trees growing a mile or two down the road.

We haul truckloads of manure, courtesy of the collective rear ends of a friend's cattle, and tons of kelp. We dig it all into the ground the way *Organic Gardening* says we should. And then we carefully lower the innocent little seeds into this mess, cover them with exactly the right amount of soil and collapse exhausted.

But is it over? Is Lucien Bouchard dating Elsie Wayne? For two months we battle with the strongest, toughest weeds this side of hell. Stephen King is interested in basing his next horror movie on the growth in my back yard. The air is as full of kamikaze (if I knew how to spell it, I would have spelt it right) mosquitoes as the ground is full of rabid chickweed.

The reward is in the harvest, right? Certainly. But I'd rather not talk about that right now because a mind can only take so much depression and stress and then it snaps. I'm not interested in snapping at this moment. Maybe later. Perhaps in September.

The question remains: why do we do it? It certainly isn't ignorance of the facts. Every year it's the same old story. No sun, no warmth, no growth. No beet, no spuds, no turnip, no carrot, no religion ...

I have a theory as to why so many of us in this fair province put ourselves through such misery on a continuing basis. Those of you interested in sociology and self-torment should follow this closely for your greater edification. Teachers of psychology, anthropology and Lamaze classes feel free to discuss this with your students when they inevitably ask about it.

Newfoundlanders and Labradorians (I know this is one time Labradorians don't want to be included with the rest of us, but them's the breaks) suffer from a terminal case of Martyr Syndrome.

Yes we do. Every last one of us. What is Martyr Syndrome? It's as simple as it's sad. It means we aren't happy unless we're suffering. The more we suffer, the happier we get, if you follow.

If society doesn't wreak enough agony and despair on us through fishery moratoria and provincial budgets, we hasten to add some of our own. We read the *Globe and Mail*. We watch Canadian-made movies on television. Or we go gardening. We will go to any lengths to make ourselves miserable.

Doubtless, there are those of you disagreeing with this thesis at this very moment. That's a silly and, given the times, rather insensitive notion, you say. Well, so it might be, but truth is truth.

Why else have we clung to this barren and fog-shrouded piece of unreal estate for the last five hundred years? Why else have we put up with poverty, indignity, isolation and the Gulf ferries? Why do we have Detroit channels on cable? And when we occasionally get the chance to leave this unadulterated vale of tears for more fertile fields, why do we keep coming back?

It's simple. It's the Martyr Syndrome. We were born to be miserable. It's in our genes, in our hearts and in our culture. We can no more escape it than Paul Martin can escape being Liberal.

You're probably wondering where this Martyr Syndrome thing came from to begin with. Actually, I'm not sure of its origins or for how long we've had it. But I do know we have it, and that's the interesting part.

I shall explain. Newfoundlanders, and Labradorians in part, have a gigantic guilt complex. The only way this tremendous burden of guilt that we carry around on our tired collective shoulders can be eased is when we are miserable, because then we feel we're paying our dues.

You don't believe me? Tune in to *Open Line* any day or night. The litany of woe would bring tears to a glass eye. The sixty-four-thousand-dollar question, of course, is what are we guilty about? What have we done that we must eternally indulge ourselves in self-flagellation?

I don't know. Could be anything from destroying the Great Auk to wiping out the Beothuks. Not one living soul left of either one, courtesy of ourselves. It's not nice to think about, which is probably why most of us don't very often.

Very clever, Smith, you're thinking, but it's really a lousy theory. More holes in it than in the average sermon. Won't stand up to even the most cursory academic scrutiny.

Okay, I accept what you say, if that's what you're saying. But if we in this province weren't born to inferiority as the sparks fly upward, tell me this.

Why do we let mainlanders cross the Gulf?

## The Evolution of Language

Language is ever-changing and evolving.

Old words die and new words are born. The computer alone has spawned almost a whole dictionary of terms unknown a generation ago.

Not just new inventions but also new situations give rise to virgin expressions that enrich our language and make it fresh and innovative. And so in the last few weeks we have been privileged to witness in our own time the birth of one of the most colourful, the most meaningful and the most symbolic of all expressions in the history of the spoken word.

The word is "bobbittize."

Six months ago it didn't exist. Today it's the buzzword for gossip columnists. Tomorrow it will take its place alongside "crap," "pantyhose" and "colourlok" as one of the more modern terms in your Funk and Wagnall's.

Perhaps you're not familiar with this newest action word in the English language. It arises, of course, from the celebrated case of one Mrs. Lorena Bobbitt who removed from her sleeping husband, one John Wayne Bobbitt, by means of a kitchen knife, most of his dickybird, as my dear grandmother used to call it.

If "bobbittize" were already in the dictionary, the entry would probably look something like this.

> **bobbittize 1** To cut off at the root; to remove with a sharp object; (she --d him with a serrated bread knife). **2** to cut off at the source; to slice in the bud. **3** to take away something unique and irreplaceable; (she -d the only romantic bone he had in his body). **4** To be vulnerable to being cut off, hence --able.]

"Bobbittize" would probably be preceded by the word "bobbitt," meaning someone who has suffered bobbittization; "He became a bobbitt after his partner's skilful ministrations."

Nature works in strange and wonderful ways. Think how much poorer the language would have been had the gentleman who underwent this process in the first place been named Fitzsimmons or Funk or Smith.

"I have been fitzsimmonsed" just doesn't have the same tragic ring to it as the pathetic "I have been bobbittized!"

"I have been funked," on the other hand, has distinct possibilities.

"Bobbittize" has taken on the kind of connotations that normally take generations to acquire. Already it has gone beyond its original meaning of last week—to cut off, to de-ego—and has gained lasting relevance in the battle of the sexes.

There is no question but that the psychological fallout of the act of bobbittizing has given women a sense of power they've been seeking for centuries. The unthinkable has been done and being done once can be done again.

The full horror of it is that bobbittizing can be done at any-time in any place, even in the very act of love and because of that every man knows there is really no protection against it. All the woman has to do now in the middle of an argument is to noncha-lantly pick up a knife, any old knife, and casually run her thumb along its edge, all the while fixing her gaze at a spot midway between the man's knees and his navel. No words need be spoken. Guaranteed, argument over.

"Bobbittize" has that strong suggestion of dark threat, a "don't-look-now-fella-but-it-could-happen-to-you" sort of thing. In short, and as John Wayne Bobbitt discovered, a soft pulling in your nether regions in the wee small hours of the morning may not always be an invitation to love.

If you want to test my theory, next time you're in a crowded room, preferably at a cocktail party, simply say the word "bobbittize" out loud just once, clearly and unmistakably, during a lull in the conversation. Observe the different reac-tions.

Women will immediately assume an air of superiority and confidence. They will smile the smile of the Mona Lisa (Dear God, you don't suppose ... Nawww. That was an ear and it belonged to Van Gogh and he cut it off himself) which says "I have a secret power that I can use anytime I want, so watch your back, Jack!" In the presence of others of their kind, women may even laugh outright and stare brazenly at your front.

Men will react quite differently. The word "bobbittize" will cause them to stiffen perceptibly. Hands will fly out of pockets as if by magic and assume a semi-protective position. This will last for several moments until they realize how silly they look. A few nervous chuckles will circulate the room and someone will make a weak attempt at a joke about Johnny Bobbitt.

"Ha ha. Poor John. A Bobbitt without a bobber. Ha ha."

This will cause uproarious and totally inappropriate laughter by the men, while the women continue to smile knowingly and stare insolently.

It is inevitable that the act of making love will never again be the same, at least for the male of the species. Instead of feeling intimate and comfortable he will now be desperately searching his day and wondering if he said or did anything to offend her. Instead of soothing and caressing, his hands will be searching the bedclothes for sharp objects. Instead of encouraging her hands to wander at will, he will want them above her head, up where he can see them. And any fool who falls asleep afterward is simply asking for trouble.

Yes, it's a new age. An age of paranoia, of suspicion and mistrust. An age where cutting remarks are the least of our worries, and where the term "to be cut off" has a whole new marital meaning. Neither language nor life nor loving can ever be the same. Once, you see, the worst a woman's fury could do was leave a man bewildered and perplexed.

Now it can leave him really stumped.

## The Twilight Zone

I've been thinking about getting older.

And wondering whether or not I should do it. Before one leaps into these things, you know, one would be well advised to consider the implications. Growing older may not be all it's cracked up to be. You need to know exactly what to expect and how to prepare for it.

Obviously, the thing to do is to ask people who are already older what it's like. To do that I had to define "older" so as to know who to include in my interviews. "Older," I decided, is anyone who thinks more about fibre than about sex. But I had to come up with another working definition because no one would admit to being in that category.

"Older" is when you discover that flirting with the opposite sex is a one-way operation. I gave up on that one because it was uncomfortably close to home.

"Older" is when your spouse rolls toward you in the early morning, reaches out with a tentative touch and says matter-of-factly, "Just checking" and goes back to sleep. But that isn't workable, either.

Finally, I got it. "Older" is when you're at a party that goes on into the wee small hours of the morning and you're having a whale of a time and you suddenly realize you're the oldest person there. That's a criterion with which I have first-hand experience. So I simply chose the oldest people at a couple of good parties I've been at recently and interviewed them accordingly.

The interviewees included one clergyman (still active), one clergyman's wife (extremely active), the vivacious friend of an extremely active clergyman's wife, one octogenarian, one pen pal from Ontario and selected members of my poker club. I should point out that most of these people were not aware they were being interviewed for this article. Some were not aware they were being talked to at all.

The following are some of the questions and answers from the interview notes. I expect some day to write a book from these notes entitled *Growing Older: Doing What Comes Naturally.* Catchy, eh?

*What to you is the best thing about growing older?*
Being able to say any damn thing I want, anytime I want. No one listens to me, anyway.
Having sex whenever I want.
Having sex whenever I can.
Being able to send grandchildren back to their parents when I get sick of them.
Sex not being so all-fired important in life.
The ten per cent discounts.
Women not hitting on me.
Watching your children make the same mistakes with their children that you made with them.
Enemas.

*What things in life become more important than sex when you're older?*
Let me see, now ...
I'm thinking, I'm thinking ...
Welllll ...
Gee whiz ...
Me pension.

*Is it different for women and men?*
All depends on how you're doing it.
All depends on who you're doing it with.

*I mean, is growing older different for women than for men?*
Yes, women last longer.

Yes, men get older quicker.

Yes, older women get bored with older men.

Yes, men stay sexy longer.

No, we all got bowels.

*What are the major disadvantages of growing older?*

Watching your husband turn into a dirty old man.

Having to learn new things, like how to use a condom (I suspect dry humour here).

Watching things droop, sag and dry up.

Having to put up with younger people.

Trying to laugh without cackling.

Bowels.

*What do you wish you had done differently in your life?*

I wish I had done to more and been done to less.

I wish I had loved more women and drunk more beer.

I wish I had voted PC in the last provincial election.

I wish I had learned to use a condom.

I wish I had loved more people and trusted fewer.

*What advice do you have for people about to get older?*

Do everything you ever wanted to do before it happens.

With that in mind, it is better to ask forgiveness than to ask permission. You get to have far more fun.

So there it is. It may or may not be significant that everyone I talked with is someone I know very well. The process of choosing interviewees may therefore be somewhat suspect. However, the answers are theirs alone without any further tampering from me, although I know you won't believe that.

Whatever, don't blame me if these comments seem a little out of whack with the traditional image of growing older.

I just asked the questions.

# Reaching Towards the Higher Self

I had this letter from Dr. Deepak Chopra, M.D.

It was one of those brochures selling personal improvement programs. You know the type: "follow these simple rules, which you can purchase from me at these new low prices, and in seven days you'll have a richer, fuller life than you ever dreamed."

I don't know if I'm the only one blessed enough to get these things or not. Perhaps they only pick those who obviously need improvement.

I tear up most of that garbage, as you probably do, too, although I did pause to glance carelessly at this one. It didn't begin much better than most.

The first line read, "You are your own reality." Well, whoop-de-do. I am my own reality, whatever the hell that means. I couldn't have had much to do that day, because I decided to try and find out.

I looked up the word "reality" in the dictionary. It means, in short, existence. So I'm my own existence. Big deal. Whose existence would I be if not my own, dear Doctor? Yours? There's a scary thought. For both of us.

What the good Doctor doesn't seem to understand is that my own reality is nothing to write home about. I can think of several people on this earth whose existence seems to be a heck of a lot better than mine: Hugh Hefner, Madonna, Bill Clinton. So what's new, pussycat.

At this point, I was about to start ripping this bullmanure into shreds when another sentence partway down the page practically leaped into my face. "Discover your inner self and you'll enjoy spontaneous fulfillment of all your desires."

Now there's something to grab the attention of any hot-blooded male. It even grabbed mine. Thinking about it, I realized I've already had some of my desires filled, and the truth is that for the most part the filling was fairly spontaneous. I suppose "fairly spontaneous" is the same as being a little pregnant. Either you are or you're not or it is or it isn't. Right? But you do understand what I mean.

All my desires? Good grief, Sir, I don't even know what all my desires are. There may be some that should never see the light of day. In fact, I'm fairly sure of it. There are some that should never see the dark of night. I'm fairly sure of that, too.

In all truth, I don't know if I could stand having all my desires filled. I'm not sure anyone else could stand it, either, particularly those with starring roles in those desires. I'm a complex individual, after all, and having all my desires filled might have strings attached. Like incarceration. Or divorce. Or homicide.

I'd be happy to have fifty per cent of all my desires filled. On reflection, make that seventy-five per cent. No point in taking a chance on missing something.

I was now fully encouraged to read on. "Discover your higher self," the letter said, "and you will find a self that is totally intelligent." Now this might be useful. I immediately made a mental note to send a copy of the letter, with this particular sentence underlined, to everyone in Confederation Building who got there via an election. There's one or two within those hallowed walls who could use a smidgen more of intelligence. Indeed, I could probably use some myself, being down a quart or two according to some of my fan mail, and I'm not in government at all. Which is only half the story.

There was another sentence in Dr. Chopra's little missive which interested me as well. "You'll glow with the freedom that comes with being able to make all the right choices while never having to make any choices at all."

Fascinating thought. Imagine never having to make choices. Never again having to choose between Aqua Velva and Brut. Between tinned beans in tomato sauce and tinned beans in pork fat and molasses. Blue tie or green. Doing it tonight, as opposed to tomorrow morning. Intriguing.

But tell me. If I don't make those kinds of important decisions, who will? Will the right can of beans automatically jump off the shelf and into my shopping cart? Will the right tie spontaneously wrap itself around my neck, fully colour coordinated and not too tight? Boggles the mind.

Actually, this got me thinking about the choices I don't make now, such as: who governs me; the price of gas; my relatives; tonight, as opposed to tomorrow morning. When you stop and think about it, who has choices anymore?

You have to admit, though, that Dr. Chopra's letter is most tempting.

"Come with me," it said, "to a new reality where all is love and lightness, bliss and unbelievable beauty." If Dr. Deepak Chopra can take Newfoundlanders into that kind of new reality, he's got my vote. I know some people who could stand some bliss right now, not to mention love and lightness. We'll all go with you, Doctor, following along like rats behind the Pied Piper of Hamlin.

Precious few of us plan to follow the government anymore. That would be more like the Pied Piper following the rats. Not much lightness and bliss in that direction.

The final clincher in Dr. Chopra's program to radically improve myself was his offer to find the "me" inside of me. You see, I always knew there was someone else in there. That's who I normally blame for these columns, my baser desires and not always being colour-coordinated. But that "me" inside of me, according to the Doctor, is nobody's fool. He knows "why you are here on earth, what you need and how to get it." Which about covers it.

Obviously, I don't know this "me" very well or I wouldn't be sitting here scratching out this rubbish in the wee small hours of the morning when I should be lying peacefully or otherwise in my bed. No doubt about it, that's obviously a "me" worth knowing. All in all, Dr. Chopra's program may be worth doing. And I have yet to tell you the best part.

For the first thirty days it's free.

## Stuff and Nonsense

S-T-U-F-F.

The letters stand for Stacks and Tons of Unusable Friggin' Folderol. That's what "stuff" is. I had to strain rather hard for that one because the double *F* is difficult to work with. Perhaps you can do better.

Other Half says that "stuff" is the bane of her existence. The house is full of it, she says, and it's making her sick, driving her crazy and otherwise annoying her something awful.

"We just have to get that stuff out of the basement," she'll pronounce, usually around five in the morning, her favourite time for pronouncements. Coincidentally, that isn't exactly the time of day I'm at my brightest and most alert and just looking for something constructive to do in the basement.

"We have to do something about the stuff in the attic," is another of her favourites, again usually delivered at the most appropriate of times—between midnight and daybreak.

"It's a wonder the ceiling doesn't fall in on us," she'll go on, as though that's the one thought that will get me up off the pillow and up into the attic.

"We simply have to get that stuff out of the bathroom."

The stuff in this case refers mostly to the vast number and variety of magazines sitting in the bathroom waiting to be carefully read rather than casually flipped through.

It is important to note here that the pronoun "we" is used by OH as the royal plural, and bears no resemblance whatever to the intended specific suggestion contained in the whole statement. The fact is that the "we" in all cases is without any doubt whatsoever to be interpreted as "you." "You" just have to ... "You" simply have to ... etc., etc.

To carry the thing a wee bit further, there is also not a shred of doubt but that the "you" is directed at "me," the "me" whose name and impressive photograph appear at the top of this column. Do you see the natural progression of both thought and pronoun here, from "we" to "you" to "me"? It's something only a wife could manage. If that's sexist, so be it.

There may be some small modicum of truth to the charge that we have too much stuff lying around the house. There's not enough room on a compact disc to itemize it all, but we can identify some of it.

Cans half full of paint, not an ounce of which has ever been used anywhere in our house so don't ask me where it came from and which cannot be thrown out because, well, we might need it to paint a birdhouse or something someday. Hardened paint brushes, to be softened up when we go to work on the birdhouse. Boxes, of all sizes and descriptions that don't hold anything now, but you never can tell. Footwear galore: boots, shoes, rubbers, sneakers, pumps, Ski-Doo boots, unemployment boots, baby boots, ski boots and on and on. No foot with a shred of dignity would ever haul on one of these things, but there's always the possibility ... Old textbooks from college days three decades ago. Clothes handed down so often they'll fit anyone. Half-broken toys, fully broken furniture, great ugly family heirlooms (from OH's side of the family), bottles, jars, containers and cake tins. I could go on and am greatly tempted to do so. But you get the idea.

The problem is that while none of this stuff is useful now, and certainly never will be useful now, all of it has the potential for unlimited use in the future. And herein lies its immeasurable value. This is the "stuff" of which tomorrows are made. This is the "stuff" that holds the future together. Without this "stuff" the future would probably never come. Nothing is as pertinent to all our tomorrows as "stuff."

It's difficult to explain this to someone whose basement looks as though no centipede has ever set one of its hairy little feet on the floor and whose closets contain only today's clothes. But that's the truth of it. Those of us who have basements, attics, bathrooms and closets full of stuff are not too lazy to throw it out. We are simply holding it in trust for another time. It's not a responsibility we take lightly.

Scientists and philosophers have stated that it is not possible to bring either the past or the future to the now, an idea which should be as clear as a Constitution debate. In other words, it is never the past and never the future, it is only now.

I have proven both science and philosophy wrong on this one, not just once but several times. I have shown that the future can come to the present with startling suddenness. It happens immediately after you throw out just one little piece of something you can see no need for now, and for which you can envisage absolutely no practical use in the future.

It doesn't happen all that often with us "stuff" purists, but when it does all the natural laws of the universe are suspended. The stuff is no sooner irretrievably in the garbage when bang! you need it immediately and in the worst possible way. I have never seen it to fail.

This is a difficult time of year for me. OH is insisting on reducing our "stuff" quota for this decade by at least ten per cent, and my parents are due in a month or so for their regular summer visit. Father takes a dim view of the stuff in my basement. It is imperative, therefore, that the stuff older than fifteen years be gotten rid of with all possible haste. But you know as well as I what will happen. I'll throw the damn stuff out, all right.

And I'll spend the rest of the summer needing it.

## Big Brother Watching Us

Want to see one of your worst nightmares unfold?

Go see the movie *Demolition Man*. Sylvester "The Stallion" Stallone is in it, but that's not the main nightmare. Sandra Bullock is in it, too, and that more than makes up for the presence of eloquent Sly.

The plot is set in the year 2032 in a great metropolitan area of Southern California. This "city" is alcohol-free, red meat-free, gun-free, smoke-free and—would you believe—salt-free. It is a crime to swear in public. It is also sex-free, which is an altogether different concept from free sex which characterized the same area a few decades ago.

Peace-loving Sylvester is set loose to combat a major and violent threat to this little Eden, and not only saves them (of course), but also ends up shaking them loose from some of their enforced sanctimony. He even manages to interest Sandra in a little old-fashioned sex (of *course*).

It's not a bad yarn, if you don't mind a wee bit of violence in your entertainment and a lot of Stallone. Personally, I prefer a wee bit of Sandra to a whole lot of Stallone, but to each his own.

The question is, where is good ole Rambo when you need him?

If our little society keeps going at its present rate and in its present direction, the city described in *Demolition Man* will by comparison look like a combination of an elementary school recess period and the Woodstock Music Festival. There's not a lot left of our lives that hasn't been hit by some regulation or other.

It's not possible to kill yourself smoking these days. Oh, smoking itself is a good way of killing yourself all right, but you're not allowed to do it. Long before lung disease, heart disease, cancer or poverty has done the job, you'll perish from exposure from having to stand outdoors at minus 30°C to grab a draw. Pneumonia and hypothermia are a far greater danger to smokers these days than nicotine ever was. I suppose stupid is stupid whichever way you want to go, but whatever happened to choice in the matter?

You may smile at the idea in the movie of red meat being banned. But I was talking to a chap from the Canadian Cancer Society the other day who assured me that in ten years red meat will be treated the same way cigarettes are now, which means, among other things, that you won't be able to afford it. It could also mean eating your steak outside on the front steps in a howling blizzard because you won't be allowed to eat red meat inside the house. I tell you it's scary.

How much longer do you think you'll have a choice between salt-free Ritz crackers and the regular? Or regular and salt-free chips? Or regular and salt-free Tums? Oh, I know they're side by side on your grocer's shelves at the moment, but if you're a salt lover, my son, I suggest you store away a hogshead or two of Windsor table salt before someone passes a law against salt shakers.

If you recall the plight of that chap out in the Goulds or wherever who isn't allowed to sell his traditional Spruce Beer anymore, you'll realize how close we are to being declared alcohol-free. In fact, the idea has already been tried in the States and the end result was an era of unprecedented violence and crime.

Prohibition also spelled the end of the Newfoundland herring fishery. You don't understand the connection? At one time Newfoundland made a tidy little sum selling herring to the States as hors d'oeuvres for drinking establishments. When Prohibition came along, poof. You don't think it could happen again? You need to listen up and have your wits about you.

I do hesitate to talk about sex. It always gets me in trouble with someone, usually OH and/or my three daughters. But OH is in other climes these days and the daughters are too embarrassed to read me anymore, so perhaps I can risk a small thought or two. Indeed, journalistic ethics demand as much. My problem is that at the moment I don't have a small thought to risk.

I don't know how we'd make the sex-free bit stick in our world, unless they found some foolproof way to discover when two or more people decide to have a go at it under the table, so to speak. Perhaps ultra sensitive sensors could be built into mattresses, shower stalls, bear rugs, chesterfields, back seats of cars, under the table, the tops of executive desks and hammocks.

You don't believe hammocks? You're right. Scratch hammocks. I don't know what I was thinking about there. Anyway, these sensors might then be hooked up to a command console somewhere, like at Cape Canaveral. Or to discourage sexual activity forever, you could simply put two or more small kids in each house.

Right up there with this stirring vision of the world of the future is the decision to close the turr season during the months that turrs are still around and can be hunted relatively safely. And let's not forget the proposed regulation to limit Newfoundlanders to five fish a day for personal consumption when we may only be able to get at the damn things for two or three days in the fall. While we're at it, this is a good time to tell all those who want to stop people from parking their trailers in the gravel pit of their choice to go to hell.

I could go on and so could you. The really scary thing is that there is no end to the numbers of people who are prepared to shower us with enough regulations to govern our lives from conception to cremation. The self-appointed guardians of our morals, manners and culture believe they are divinely sent to do just that.

You know what to tell them.

Ah well, not to worry. The way our economy is going, within a dozen years or so there'll be so few of us left on The Rock that no one will bother with what we're doing, anyway.

And you thought it was all bad!

## To Soothe the Savage Breast

Researchers in California have made a truly amazing discovery.

One of the amazing things about it is that it has nothing to do with sex. Perhaps you've noticed, as I have, that practically all the outstanding breakthroughs in recent years have had to do with sex.

Take, for example, the discovery of the G-spot. True, it was no sooner found than it was lost again, but millions will acknowledge the challenge of the search. Then there was the invention of the X-rated video, a giant step forward from dirty postcards, and the glow-in-the-dark condom.

Science in the last few years seems to have been preoccupied with improving our lot in the realm of the sensuous, and few have criticized them for it. Well, I have, of course, but I'm just one small voice in a universe of passionate acquiescence. Of course I know what I just said. I have a dictionary.

The discovery of which I speak has to do with intelligence and the way we learn. You've heard of Mozart? Mozart was composing classical music at the age of six. God knows what he was doing at the age of seven. But he wasn't much older when his father took him all over Europe as a child prodigy, playing his compositions before packed houses. Mozart was the kind of rare genius that comes along perhaps once every century.

What's all this got to do with the price of tobacco in Lab City?

Well, a team of scientists in sunny California have discovered through extensive experimentation that listening to the music of Mozart increases one's intelligence as measured on a Stanford-Binet IQ test. Not a word of a lie.

I won't go into the details of the experiment here, mainly because I didn't understand them, but there seems to be no doubt that this is so. It has something to do with the fact that Mozart was also a gifted mathematician and this carries over into the patterns of his music which seems to stimulate the neural pathways in the brain into new and vastly creative directions.

I told you I didn't understand it.

The tests were done with adults and the effects lasted for only a few hours. Now they have the idea that perhaps by exposing very young children to Mozart's compositions, the positive effect on learning ability may last a lifetime. Anyway, the experiments are continuing with that as the hypothesis.

You have to admit that this is fascinating stuff. Perhaps not right up there with G-spots and videos, but nevertheless fascinating. Imagine increasing your child's IQ by having her listen to tapes of classical music. Eat your heart out, Charlie Pride.

My little mind went to work on this phenomenon with a will, and all sorts of interesting scenarios popped up before me. If listening to classical music increases your learning ability, for example, what would be the effect of exposing oneself to the *Homebrew* radio show every day for a week?

You don't know the *Homebrew* show? Shame on you. It plays Newfoundland music all morning every morning. So I ask again, what would hearing repeated renditions of "Aunt Martha's

Sheep" do to the average brain? I know what hearing it once does to mine, but perhaps I'm not normal. Would repeated doses of "The Squid Jiggin' Ground" make one a better squid jigger? Or a better Change Islander? I'm only asking.

Perhaps you remember the movie *10*. Bo Derek played a saucy little thing who got so totally turned on by the music of "Bolero" that she wanted to make love to it all night. To be more precise, she wanted to make love to Dudley Moore all night in time to the music of "Bolero," and did. All night.

Dudley was probably asleep. "Bolero" has got to be the most boring composition ever put to music.

Nevertheless, the question to be asked here is this: "Does listening to 'Bolero' make women become more passionate lovers?" To date, I've worn out three cassette tapes, two LPs and a compact disc trying to find the answer. I wish I could tell you the results but OH won't let me.

A friend and I were talking about all of this, and he wondered what the effect of punk rock or acid rock or whatever the latest "rock" sound is, might be on your average teenager. I mention this only because he will be quite upset if I don't credit him with the idea for this column in the first place. Union local presidents are so sensitive.

Anyway, you will agree that if the opposite of black is white, the opposite of wet is dry and the opposite of Grimes is Efford (I'm really sorry, gentlemen, over the distressing frequency with which you keep cropping up in this column, but everyone enjoys a good laugh now and then), then the opposite of Mozart is punk—or whatever—rock.

So, if listening to Mozart increases the learning capacity of the brain, what would one expect listening to rock music does to that same organ? You don't know?

Listen to me carefully, now, and we'll find the answer to that question together. Do you have a teenager in the house? Good. Does that teenager listen to hours of outrageously loud and outrageously vile acid-type rock? Good. Take a moment right now to go have a good look at your offspring, a good long look ...

Are you back? Excellent. After due consideration of the state of hair, state of dress, state of mind and appetite of the fruit of your loins, can you now tell me the answer to the question of what happens to his brain?

Thought so.

## Pet Wellness

I must listen more to CBC Radio's *Crosstalk*.

Unfortunately, the program's time period of immediately after lunch doesn't often coincide with either my office hours or my travel times. But every blue moon or so I'm on the road in the middle of the day and I tune in. It really is one of my favourite radio programs and, lately, it's been even more entertaining than usual.

The last time I listened in they were talking about how to get the taste of moose and turrs off moose and turrs. Some of you will recall "The View's" response to that one, and thank you to all who wrote or called in that connection.

Then a few days ago I managed to catch *Crosstalk* again. This time they had a guest veterinarian discussing with callers such timely topics as the importance of maintaining good health in your pets. Nothing wrong with that. Cats can get as sick as the rest of us. So can dogs. Sicker. I know. I'm the one who cleans up the carpet after.

Anyway, we tuned in on the middle of a really fun conversation with a caller whose major concern was the fact that his cat was doing a fair amount of throwing up. OH has one of the weaker stomachs in the Western Hemisphere, and talk of this sort only four or five hours before supper didn't go over real well. Health care would not be her choice of professions. Sick people tend to make her, well, sick.

Veterinary medicine isn't exactly her cup of tea, either. When the talk turned to a combination of fur balls and vomit, OH covered her ears with both hands and made can't-be-repeated comments about the CBC, cats and cat owners generally. Fortunately, our granddaughter was asleep and did not overhear the running commentary from her normally discreet and dignified grandmother.

Daughter Number Two in the back seat was in stitches over her mother's reaction to cat vomit and the like. Apart from that, the subject was just a bit boring for me. But I perked up considerably, I can tell you, when they started talking about the best way to brush a dog's teeth. Brush a dog's teeth? With a toothbrush?

Yes Sir and yes Ma'am, that's exactly what they were saying. It seems that those of us who own dogs and/or cats and who aren't giving them a regular brushing are guilty of pet neglect. Nobody on the show said that, but I can read between the lines. So I started thinking about it. Before I finished thinking I was sicker than OH.

Consider the practical implications. Brushing one's teeth involves a fair amount of spitting. How do you get a dog to spit? I've never seen a dog spit. Even dogs that can fetch and sit up can't spit. I've never seen a dog rinse or gargle, either. And let's not even think about flossing. These questions were simply not addressed. They weren't even asked by the radio audience. I would have called in and asked myself, but I don't have a car phone. Just as well.

My uncles in St. Anthony used to have a dog pen under the Gully Bank. You people in St. John's and Corner Brook don't know what or where the Gully Bank is? No odds. There are people in St. Anthony who don't know where Symes Bridge or Lomond Street are, either, and don't want to know, so fair's fair.

Anyway, my uncles had this pen where they kept their dogs during the summer. Seven or eight of these beasts could strip a full-grown cow to the bone before you could say a short moo. One of my favourite pastimes as a boy was stabbing flatfish in the cove and throwing them one by one into the dogpen. I never did see the smallest bit of fish ever hit the ground.

So I have this vivid picture in my head of one of my uncles entering the pen with a tub of toothpaste and a large brush and sticking his hand in the mouth of one of those creatures in an attempt to brush its teeth.

He would have tried only twice, of course. When both arms were torn off at the shoulder sockets he'd have had to give it up. By that time, both legs would be gone, too, and the future wouldn't be looking that bright. Which may be one of the reasons neither of my uncles ever tried it, at least to my knowledge.

Come on now, people. Brushing the teeth of animals?! I thought dogs and cats and chickens and such took care of their own teeth, same as I have to do. I thought that's why we gave bones to the dogs and let cats catch birds. And I do have to tell you the truth here. Each one of my dogs' teeth will fall out on the floor and be lost in the dust of the centuries before I get to the point of brushing one yellow fang.

I'm sorry, vets and animal rights people from Hong Kong to Vancouver, but that's the way it is. I wouldn't hurt one of the little critters for the world but I have my limitations in the field of animal health care and we just reached them. I'm not going to pay anyone else to do it, either.

At the end of the program someone mentioned health care insurance for animals. With that, we leaped well past my personal limitations and into the area of general disbelief. I was pleased to hear the good doctor, who I'm sure is an excellent veterinarian, state that she thought it was a waste of money. Good stuff.

Better, she went on, to open up a bank account and put aside fifteen or twenty dollars a week to take care of pet contingencies, presumably such as dentures and root canals. But I'm not going to do that, either.

I'm still trying to find money to take care of me.

## Bloodsport

"Doe, a deer, a female deer ..."

You all know the song. Lots of female deer in Newfoundland. Caribou are members of the deer family, you know, and a doe is a doe is a doe. A female moose, on the other hand, is a cow which means moose are closer to the cattle clan than the deer crowd. Otherwise a male moose would be called a stag, which it isn't. A male caribou isn't called a bull which, in terms of gender, it is.

Confusing? Yes. Important? Nah.

We were talking about does.

Father and I had a caribou licence this year. That's how Father discovered there are roughly five hundred times as many does in the province as there are stags. We, you see, had a "stag only" licence.

Perhaps five hundred times as many is a bit of an exaggeration, although not to hear Father tell it. For three days running on the edge of the Gaff Topsails, Father saw more does than he could shake a stick at and nary a stag among them.

We got to talking about it one night, the four of us. Father said the caribou situation was reflective of the human condition where the males, like the good, die young, while the females, having less stress in their lives, grow comfortably old.

Other Half took exception to that.

"If the stags do in fact die young," she said, "it's because of greed. They die of exhaustion trying to service a whole herd of does, and when they're not busy procreating they're battling it out with other stags for the right to even more females. In that respect," OH went on with some heat (no pun intended), "they are indeed a lot like men: unwilling to share and trying to get it all done in a jiffy."

"That reminds me of a joke," I broke in, trying to defuse the situation. "An old bull and a young bull were standing on a hill looking down on a herd of cows. The young bull turned to the old bull and said—"

"You're right," said my mother to OH. "The male caribou work so hard fighting and mating that the meat is not fit to eat after September. And men are not fit to live with after forty."

This last delivered with a meaningful glance at my father.

"Well!" said Father, "Well!"

Again I broke in.

"So the young bull says to the old bull, 'Let's run down the hill and make love to a couple of those cows.' And the old bull replied ..."

OH was glaring at me.

"You're not telling a dirty story in front of your mother, are you?"

"Of course not. It's just cute, that's all, and it's related to what you and Mother are saying about stags and men."

"I thought we were talking about does and women," said Father.

"The reason women live longer than men," said OH, "is that they're more durable and they don't go through life wasting their energies on trying to be the best in everything."

"Nonsense!" snorted Father. "Rubbish! Women have a much easier time of it and so don't wear out as fast."

"AND," I said quickly, "the old bull said to the young bull, 'No, my friend, let's walk down the hill and make love to them all.'"

There was a small silence. I tried to explain.

"The young bull wanted to run down the hill, you see, and the old bull suggested they walk down the hill and conserve their energy."

OH was not impressed.

"I think it's a bit of an off-colour story," she said, "especially for your mother."

"And," added Mother, "it's as old as the hills."

I forget where the conversation went from there.

As I was saying, Father hunted for almost the whole week and saw only does. Since I was working and unavailable, he took with him each time a son-in-law (mine) for company and assistance. Let's just say that the arrangement didn't work out that well. Father called them all jinxers and vowed to go by himself next time.

Mother felt strongly that he should not go hunting alone at his age.

"A man approaching eighty years of age," she said, "should not be up on the Gaff Topsails hunting caribou all by himself."

At the end of the week she was pretty fed up herself.

"Enough of this foolishness," she said. "Tomorrow I'm going with him."

We all tried hard not to smile. Mother was obviously forgetting that she and Father would bounce off eighty at about the same time.

But next morning off they went after leaving the details of exactly where they planned to hunt so that we'd know where to go look if they weren't back on time.

They were. With the four quarters of as fine a stag as you'd want to see. Mother described it all dramatically, if a little succinctly.

"All of a sudden there he was," she said excitedly, "standing right in the middle of the road! I jumped out and waved a white sheet to distract him, and that gave your father time to get his rifle and find his bullets and take a shot. He didn't miss."

Neither of them, God bless 'em, misses very much.

## The Noblest Profession

Sometime ago, someone called me an outstanding journalist.

That was nice and I appreciated it. Fact is, it was also wrong. I had no objection to the "outstanding" bit, mind you. Indeed, I will admit to some smidgen of truth in "outstanding." "Outstanding" and I are not total strangers. Not really.

But when you call me a journalist you confuse me with Daughter Number Three, which is rather difficult since she's young, blond and female and I'm none of it. She is also a journalist. I am not. I am a columnist. What's the diff? Be prepared to beam aboard, Jerry.

This column will someday find its way into journalism textbooks as the definitive word on the difference. Why do I think you want to read about it now? Haven't the slightest. I know I want to write about it now so looks like you're stuck.

As a columnist, I can write what I think. On second thought, if I always wrote what I think my editors would fire me, my family would disown me and my wife would divorce me. That isn't quite true, either. One of the reasons OH has stuck with me through thick and thin is the way I think. I'm just not allowed to write about what I think about. That's not entirely accurate, either, because I do think about what I write about. I just don't always write about some of the things I think about. If I did, I'd be rich and famous. Lonely, of course, but rich and famous. I trust I've made myself clear.

Perhaps we should try this again. A columnist writes opinion, usually his own. I use the male pronoun "his" because I'm thinking mostly about me. It's a habit I have—thinking mostly about me, I mean. It is also a distinguishing characteristic of columnists generally, because it takes a very egocentric person to believe that other people are the least bit interested in your opinion. It adds even more to one's conceit that editors will actually pay you to express your opinion in public. God bless 'em, every one.

A columnist expresses his own thoughts and opinions on anything that interests him. He has few restrictions or parameters, other than those imposed by common decency and libel laws, and as long as he keeps his readers interested and tuned in, he's fine. So is she, if the columnist happens to be female.

The journalist, whether print, radio or television, is another species of animal entirely. In her case, personal opinion is a no-

no. I use the female pronoun "her" because I'm thinking about Daughter Number Three, which is another habit I have— thinking about Daughter Number Three, I mean. I'm into the habit of thinking about all my children, of course, but Daughter Number Three is the only journalist in the family at the moment and so merits special consideration under this topic.

Perhaps we're getting a little sidetracked here. Journalists are bound by all manner of rules and conventions that make the practice of this profession not only difficult, but often scary. They deal only with fact and truth, for example, but the reality that fact and truth are not always congruent can sometimes get newspeople, and those on whom they are reporting, into hot water.

The manner in which facts are presented can twist or even deny the truth of the situation. For example, don't tell your wife you think she's a great cook while staring raptly at an erotic dancer. Both you and truth will suffer.

Journalists must have a sense of responsibility to their readers and to the people making the news. They must be careful not to sensationalize or "create" news from what is mundane or trivial. They have an obligation not to stir up people or spread alarm through the public simply for the sake of having a good story. Manure-disturbers do not make good journalists. On the other hand, they make excellent columnists, which most of you already knew.

The columnist writes to entertain, to titillate, to amuse, to cheer up and sometimes to enlighten. The keywords are creativity and flexibility. The journalist writes only to inform, as accurately, precisely and responsibly as possible. The keywords are discipline and integrity. Which is not to say, of course, that reporters and newspeople aren't creative, or that columnists don't have integrity. We're talking emphasis and focus here. I thought you knew that.

The greatest difference between columnists and journalists is that people believe what the newsperson says is accurate. In fact, people believe it whether it is true or not. They don't have much choice since integrity in journalism is something we have to assume. No one expects a columnist to tell the truth because precious few of us do.

There are good columnists and good journalists. There are those in both groups who are not. Bad columnists will simply bore you to death if you let them (you still with me here?). As far as their views are concerned, you can take them or leave them. Up to you. The bad newsperson is a highly dangerous being. By accident or design, he or she has the potential to destroy careers and reputations, help bring down governments and generally cause havoc with individuals and society alike.

As a columnist, I have great respect for newspeople of all types. For me, journalism vies with teaching and healing as the noblest profession, and journalists deserve the same dignity and respect we seem to offer those others as a matter of course. Columnists don't ask for dignity and respect.

Columnists ask for more money.

## Inning Management

I can't wait for baseball season to start.

The vast intelligence constantly being paraded by professional baseball figures is truly fascinating. For sheer creative genius the "boys of summer" personalities are unrivalled in the world of entertainment.

Listen to almost any interview with a coach or player, or follow the commentary for a few innings, and you'll see what I mean. This year I plan to watch every game with my trusty notebook and pen in my lap so that these jewels of wisdom and insight can be recorded for posterity, you being posterity. I hope you don't mind.

Anyway, the season opened just today, and I already have one of the all-time great baseball brain buster ideas ever. It's called "Inning Management" or IM.

You've never heard of Inning Management? Neither had I until now, but I'll try to explain it. It's a bold new game strategy so subtle and yet so obvious one wonders why no one has thought of it before.

How does it work? I'd like to put it in simple terms but this concept simply defies everyday language. The announcers were struggling with it during the Expos-Jays exhibition game last week and finally had to rely on the direct wording of the genius who thunk it up, as I must do now.

The idea is rather complicated, as you might expect, but it goes something like this; in fact, it goes exactly like this: if your team gets a run scored against it in any given inning, you must try not to have any more runs scored against you in that same inning. That's straight from the measureless mind of one of the Expos coaches. He figures it will revolutionize the game and practically guarantee them a pennant. Deceptively simple, eh?

But don't be fooled, folks. This is heavy stuff. You may want to think about it for a while and ponder the implications. I have and it's frightening.

What do you suppose will happen to the Jays if other teams in the majors start taking that idea seriously? As soon as the boys get a run across the plate the other team will practice "Inning Management" and try and prevent them from getting another one. The Jays may have no choice but adopt the same measures in self-defence. Next thing you know all the teams are doing it and the game of baseball as we know it is lost and gone forever.

Suppose the same principle holds for other sports as well. If a hockey team gets a goal scored against it in the first period, for example, this creative new strategy would dictate that the team try not to have a second goal scored against it in the same period. What would that do to the game from a spectator point of view? How would the San Diego Sharks or the Idaho Spuds or the Toronto Maple Leafs cope?

I firmly believe that the current NHL strike is over that very question. No one, of course, is willing to say that and you can't blame them. This stuff is dynamite.

Apply the IM principle to figure skating and look what happens. The skater who falls in her program makes a valiant effort not to fall again for the whole performance. Imagine what the Olympics figure skating would have been like had they known about Inning Management. Let some of those Russian and European coaches get hold of that idea and we've seen the last figure skating champion from this side of the Atlantic.

It is innovative thinking such as this that has put professional sports where they are today, and it's time the rest of society was willing to learn from them. At the risk of sounding subversive, let's see where an application of the IM principle to life in general could take us. This may sound a little farfetched and even ridiculous to some, but most great ideas do in their infancy. String bikinis, for example.

In politics, if you lost an election this year, you would try hard not to lose another election for the rest of the year. You might, if you were so inclined, try not to lose another election for the rest of your life.

In business, if you lost a dollar today you would desperately try not to lose another dollar in the same time period. Conversely, in private life if you spent a dollar today you would try hard to keep the same thing from happening until at least tomorrow. We'd have fewer people in debt if society adopted the Inning Management idea.

In the area of human behaviour the IM principle works even better. If you acted like a horse's patootie today you would try hard not to act that way again for the rest of the year.

The great guru of baseball intelligence is Yogi Berra. His Diet Pepsi line, "If it's so popular, why is everyone drinking it?" is typical of many of his comments down through the years as player and coach. It was Yogi, for example, who came up with such all-time classics as, "It ain't over till it's over," and "I've got just three words for you, fella, 'Bug off.'" This is the same kind of creative thinking that gives us "Inning Management."

I predict that "Inning Management" will revolutionize and revitalize not only baseball but all sports and perhaps all of living. I plan to explain to you how it can even brighten up your sex life.

Just as soon as I figure it out myself.

## Down to the Sea

Did I go fishing last weekend?

Wasn't it the first of only four weekends this year Newfoundlanders are allowed on the salt water to catch cod for their own personal use? Exactly. So what do you think? Exactly.

Twenty, in answer to the next question. We caught twenty fish. When we're allowed to take ten cod each you might think that's some kind of coincidence. It would be if there were only two in the boat. But there were four of us so we were allowed to take forty. We got twenty.

We got two that were barely large enough to be called cod, two that could be called very small cod and sixteen adolescent tomcods. OH and I would normally run through four of these at a single breakfast sitting.

One weekend down, three to go in the great cod roulette fishing fiasco.

We set out in the wee small hours of a Saturday pre-dawn. My crew consisted of a son, a son-in-law and a nephew. I was captain. It said so on my white captain's cap that my mother gave me last Christmas.

The plan was to be on the water before six. The crew member who does not reside in this house was banging on the door at five-twenty. Luckily I was up, which helped consolidate my authority as captain.

Since we planned to be on the water for a good five or six hours a bit of a lunch seemed a necessity. In my grandfather's day that was usually hardtack and a bottle of cold water. My own father had stepped up to molasses bread and cold water. I had evolved to molasses bread and a thermos of hot tea. I asked Nephew what he had in his pack for lunch.

"Bagels," he said. "Bagels with raisins."

Bagels? With raisins? I associate bagels with tea parties and cream puffs. With midmorning coffee breaks in the secretarial pool. Bagels go with squid bait and guts and slime the way petticoats and lace go with Hulk Hogan. A fishing mug-up is a hard-tack scene. I knew immediately we had problems that might challenge my captaincy at the outset.

It's a long leap from hard bread and cold water to bagels, far more than the separation of four generations of fishing can explain. What kind of seaman takes bagels out on the bosom of the North Atlantic Ocean?

I sized up this particular seaman in his cut-off jean shorts, his unlaced sneakers, his "Woodstock Two" T-shirt and recognized that in this particular case bagels might not be entirely inappropriate.

The remaining crew was summoned from slumber. Son had been at an all-night barbecue and hadn't gotten in until four-thirty. He did not look spry.

Son-In-Law looked wary. He had fished with me before and knew that the crew got all the dirty jobs, like gutting fish and cutting up squid bait left over from last year and getting squid juice over his clothes. That knowledge seemed to dampen his spirits somewhat, but he wasn't about to back out. I recognized another potential challenge to my command.

I instructed the crew to grab a slice of bread and a cup of tea while I was pulling on my long johns in the bedroom. Since dawn had not yet cracked, I had to turn on the bedroom light to make sure I put the things on properly.

It is most irritating when having to heed a minor call of nature a mile or two offshore in a small open boat to find that your long johns are on backwards. The minor call which can normally be answered with the discreet use of a bailing bucket then becomes a major problem which can only be resolved through heading directly for the nearest point of land and finding a clump of bushes. That, or hanging over the side of the vessel and mooning the jellyfish.

My loving wife greeted the turning on of the bedroom light with the kind of remark that does not speak well for a long-term relationship. I recognized a distinct lack of respect for my seafaring position.

Suddenly I smelled something. Something that reminded me of campfires and girl scouts (I had never been a boy scout). I rushed out to the kitchen to see who was burning what and found my crew having a wiener roast.

"Got to have breakfast, my son," said my son defensively. I noted the "my son." Obviously, another mark of disrespect to naval authority.

Nephew suggested that the bagels might go well with the wieners, and Son-In-Law felt that a slice or two of toast wouldn't go astray and did we have any bacon, because if we had some bacon we could have some bacon and eggs, too, if we had any eggs.

It was time to exercise some firm discipline, as captains have had to do for hundreds of years before me, and within the half-hour we were cruising out beautiful Shoal Arm looking for the fish that everyone says are not there.

We spent six hours on the water on the kind of splendidly beautiful day that this year we have come to expect as our due. We had to go ashore only once because I had turned off the light too quickly while putting on my long johns, and while ashore we sat on some logs and ate our lunch and threw rocks at dead things and, all in all, had a great morning.

The fishing wasn't great, but it was well spread out among the crew. One chap who prefers to remain anonymous caught mostly sculpin, another did well on the rock cod, and the bagel kid turned out to be the highliner in both size and quantity, closely followed by Son.

The relative positions of Captain and Son-In-Law are not to be discussed. I have to admit one thing, though.

The bagels weren't half bad.

## Memories Are Made of This

I was just looking around my office.

It doesn't take long. Actually, it's a combination of office-storage room-den-catchall type place with little to recommend it except it's mine. But it does hold all sorts of knick-knacks and things pinned, nailed and glued to the walls to remind me of those tremendously interesting occasions in my life which I would otherwise forget. This includes a thousand and one mementoes from groups to whom I've "guest-spoken" over the years.

Normally, I race down the stairs on Sunday nights (I'm in the basement) conscious only of the fact that I've put off my column till the last minute again. Then I sit at the computer and stare desperately at the screen until inspiration strikes. Many of you will be surprised to know that it doesn't always happen.

Rarely do I take the time to scrutinize the paraphernalia that surrounds me like a padded cell. But tonight I did, and found myself looking back to some of my more memorable speaking engagements.

There, for example, is the program from a high school graduation I attended a few years ago as guest speaker. Someone either intentionally or innocently—I have my opinion—filled all the sugar bowls on the head table with salt.

The first inkling anyone had that something was wrong was when the wife of one of the clergy present spit up all over the table. It was quite a sight. She was joined almost immediately by the principal, the MC for the evening and numerous others. The whole length of the head table sounded as though we were in a tobacco spitting contest at the Long Branch Saloon with everyone's mouth on automatic. OH thought it was hilarious, but of course she doesn't take sugar.

Here's a little pin they gave me for speaking at a rather sophisticated "do" of business professionals in one of our major cities. OH, at my insistence, dressed to the nines and went with me. As we parked outside the entrance to this place, she noticed that people were going in the door as they had come into the world, one by one. No couples, no pairs.

"Either every marriage in this part of the Island is on the rocks," said OH, "or this affair doesn't include spouses."

"Don't be silly," I said, "all banquets include spouses and significant others."

"Not this one," she said, "and I'm not going in there until you check it out for sure."

For some reason or other OH is sensitive about being where she's not wanted.

So I checked it out for sure and I was wrong. OH sat in the car in the parking lot for the two and a half hours it took to get through the evening's proceedings, getting hungrier and more steamed by the minute. There are one hundred and fifty minutes in two and one half hours. At the end of them she was very hungry, and exceedingly steamed. Since then, she accompanies me to such affairs only when an invitation in her name, sworn out before a Justice of the Peace, is hand-delivered to the house two weeks before the date in question. I can't blame her.

I have another little program from another school graduation which says in bold print that I, Ed Smith, am the MC, as I was asked to be several weeks in advance.

As we sat down to dinner, the principal of the school leaned over and whispered, "This is a bit embarrassing, but there's a small error on the program. You're not the MC."

"That's okay," I whispered back. "Don't be embarrassed on my account. I'll just relax and enjoy the evening. But perhaps I shouldn't sit at the head table."

"Yes, you should," he replied. "You're the guest speaker."

Also stuck in my wall is a pin from a well-known professional group which hired me as an after-dinner speaker for a very momentous occasion. Since I spent hours in preparation, lost two days out of my life going and coming, and since they could afford it, I charged them the full fee. No problem with fees, they said, to get someone of my calibre and for such an occasion. Prepare to speak to about two hundred and fifty. Right.

The big night arrived and with it seven people, counting OH and me. Perhaps there were more than seven, but not much. Seems a similar group was having a similar function on the other side of town with a better speaker, and couple by couple, everyone jumped ship without declaring their intentions to the organizers. I suggested we join them, but my group got stubborn and demanded not only that we stay put, but also that I give them the speech they had paid for. I have known jollier occasions.

There are no mementoes in this room or anywhere in this world of the time I performed at a rally in St. John's Town on the night of October 29. October 29 is our wedding anniversary, which is bad enough. This particular October 29 was our Silver Anniversary. By the time I realized what I had done it was too late to cancel.

OH spent much of that evening sitting in the car and making plans for my eternal damnation. She has destroyed all evidence of the occasion, and from what I understand from her female friends I, or vital parts of me, am fortunate not to have disappeared with the evidence. Happily, the incident was pre-Bobbitt.

So you think traipsing around the country every weekend to speak to various and demanding audiences is fun? That I get a tremendous kick out of it? I've got news for you, friend.

You're right.

## Turnaround

I don't know if you saw *Maclean's* a few weeks ago.

One article featured a picture of a woman being hauled asunder by a couple of youngsters on her right and an elderly couple on her left pulling with might and main on her arms. She looked like a wishbone in a dress.

The story in question was all about this poor person and the "sandwich" generation to which she apparently belongs, torn between having to care for kids on the one hand and aging parents on the other. The gist of the article was that the responsibility for both is just too much for people in this day and age. Indeed, it was shown to be one of Canada's most pressing social problems.

I read the article carefully and learned several things about dealing with older people, especially if they happen to be your parents. The article didn't exactly say what I'm about to, mind you, but the conclusions were obvious to me and I'm satisfied to share them with you.

Old people can be a bloody nuisance, sitting around the house taking up space. Sometimes they drool when they eat and sometimes they won't eat at all. Just like youngsters.

They have the most unreasonable expectations, too, like wanting to talk to you when you don't want to talk to them, and expecting a response. Just like youngsters.

And don't say old people can't be thoughtless. My own parents are seventy-five and instead of acting like old people and sitting home and rocking, they're always off on fishing expeditions and hunting trips, dragging an old trailer behind an even older Chevy. Think they'll settle down so we don't have to worry about them? Not on your sweet pension cheque.

My father especially is a proper nuisance. I buy a boat and he wants to build the windshield for it and paint it and buy little things to make it look good. Plain interference.

This fall he'll want Son and me to go moose hunting with him for a few days, walking through the autumn woods and the three of us having a scattered mug-up by a brook or pond. He'll want to tell stories of hunts long past, and Son will rather listen to him than clean out the frying pan.

OH's father is just as bad. No point in starting up a conversation with him, because no matter what the topic, he knows more about it than I do, and he has me tied up in verbal knots in less time than it takes to tell it. No way will he just sit there and talk vaguely about the past, like he's supposed to. I've never even heard him sing a hymn about going Home.

It's impossible to have a decent social life with old people around. OH and I once organized a memorable scavenger hunt for a party we threw. My PU's (parental units) were visiting at the

234 ■ ED SMITH

time and wouldn't stay in the bedroom out of the way. In fact,
Father got elected by some naive soul to sit in a large chair and
record the items being rushed in by each team.

We were and are a rather competitive little group, and the
scavenger list contained some rather interesting items that
required people to go into strange places and do strange things,
all within a specified time limit.

When we talk about that night, as we still do with some
delight, the stories revolve around the chap who broke his ankle
falling into a ditch but whom no one would stop to help; the
woman who ran into a local hotel to steal a menu, and knocked
herself senseless against the glass door; and last but by no means
least, the look on my clergyman father's face as people rushed into
the room and threw into his unsuspecting lap used pampers from
a local baby, used panties from a local waitress and (no comment)
condoms from a local party.

You see, parents spoil everything.

The best thing is to have nothing to do with parents once they
reach sixty. Either move away or buy a new lock for your door and
change your phone number. Once you get involved with them, old
parents are the real dickens to get rid of. They keep hanging
around as if you had nothing better to do than spend time with
them.

Be aware of the guilt trip, too. So what if they took fifteen
to twenty of the best years of their lives to wipe your nose
and other less savoury parts of your anatomy. So what if they
bled themselves dry funding your various enterprises, and
worried themselves sick about everything from measles to
matrimony. You didn't ask to be born and you owe them
nothing. You certainly don't owe them the best years of your
life.

If by now you haven't realized the real tone of this column you're too damned stun to be reading anything, and that's a fact.

Look, I'm sure that elderly parents can be an absolute trial for even the most well-meaning person. I know, too, that often the most loving children just can't cope with the demands of caring for sick parents, and that this is a national problem.

But so can your children be a trial and a hell on earth in certain situations. You take what you get in both instances and do the best you can with it.

The thing is, older people can be and usually are an enrichment to your life and a joy in your home. I think what offended me most about the article in question was that it didn't say that at all. Old people were seen simply as a problem to their grown children.

Which, of course, we never were to them.

## The End Cometh

The end of time is imminent.

That's what an old friend told me the other day. Actually, she's a friend who's quite old. There's a difference, you know.

But she firmly believes it, bless her heart, and she's not alone. The government is obviously thinking along the same lines.

That isn't exactly what my friend said, though.

Her actual words were, "We'm about to witness the return o' the Lard." The world has gone all to hell, she said, and The End is near.

Truth is, she didn't say "hell," either. She'd be roasting in it before she ever said it. But "hell" is an accurate translation. What

she meant was that the arse is gone clean out of 'er. Her feeling
was that she could vomit at what's goin' on. It's all screwed, blued,
tattooed and shampooed. Of course she never said any of it in
those words. She's not the type. Far too dignified for that. I'm not,
so I'm pleased and delighted to have the privilege of interpreting
for her.

She's right, you know. We're closer to The End than we ever
were. If it's going to happen at all, we're closer to it now than we
were yesterday. Chronologically, if not theologically, that can't be
argued. And some day in some way the end is likely to come. My
bet is that it's immediately after the budget comes down.

Anyway, it all reminds me of an incident from my younger
days that may hold a parallel to the present provincial financial crisis, given the upcoming budget and all. By the time you
read this, of course, it'll all be over. But the revelations of
John the Divine on the Island of Patmos have nothing on this
stuff.

I once lived in an area of the province much frequented by
raving fundamentalists. I use "raving" in the demented sense.
Their clergyman, if I may use the word loosely, was a chap much
given to frightening the hell out of his flock with dramatic revelations of the afterlife, especially that part of it prepared for the
"unsaved." Needless to say he attracted large congregations of
unsaved every Sunday night.

People like to hear there's a chance they may be going to hell.
It gives them a great adrenalin rush similar to what the insane get
when they jump off 400 foot high bridges dangling from a bungee
cord. I call it the Evel Knievel syndrome and it's common in your
hellfire-and-brimstone type Christian. Nothing more exciting
than knowing you've been saved from perdition in the nick of
time.

Then one blessed Sabbath evening in early fall, the pastor gave his flock a wonderful Christmas present.

The End would come, he announced, in a great baritone voice designed to reach The Other Side itself, on January 1 at the crack of dawn. It would be, he cried, the last time dawn so cracked, although these may not have been his exact words.

The faithful went wild. People made preparations for the end, like you would if you could. Prompted by fear and guilt, not to mention their pastor, they gave large amounts of money to the church.

There was some question among those sitting in the seats of the scornful as to whether cash would still be legal tender in the days following The End, but none of the flock stopped to think much about that. Truth was, while they might sing lustily about it and pray earnestly for it not many were really that anxious for the return o' the Lard. Joy over the prospect was not the immediate response of the faithful.

Christmas wasn't exactly stress-free that year. Instead of toys and aftershave lotion and perfume, people gave their children and each other bibles and prayer books. Men stopped cutting wood for the winter. Where some of them were going it would be quite warm enough. Women stopped darning socks and washing clothes. Clothes would be superfluous in the sweet by-and-by, they said.

Some fishermen didn't bother to haul up their boats before freeze-up. Boats wouldn't be needed to cross over Jordan.

Finally it was December 31, the night to end all nights. A night of snow and wind. A fitting night to herald Judgment Day. The faithful crowded into the tabernacle and set up a wailing of singing and praying that would put the idea of ending it all in the Almighty's mind had it never been there before.

I wasn't there myself, but I did hear afterward that precious few of those prayers were for the unsaved who were home watching the Ed Sullivan Show. Crass as it may be, people have a tendency in those situations to think only of themselves. Sad, really.

Inevitably dawn approached. And then it cracked. Or to be more precise, it rumbled. With the first faint streak of light came a crashing crescendo that got louder and louder and closer and closer until it was practically on top of them.

The congregation went into collective hysterics. Some huddled into fetal positions and pulled their coats over their heads. Others dove under the seats. It wasn't much of a welcoming party for Whoever was meeting them from the Other Side.

History has failed to record what the pastor himself was doing at the time. The scornful suggested he was in his office counting the night's collections. I like to think he was looking fearlessly and with great faith out the window to be the first to see the approaching apocalypse.

And if he was, he did. Thing is, nowhere in apocalyptic literature had it been foretold that Armageddon would come in the form of a labouring Department of Highways snowplow making an awful racket hauling its heavy blade over a rough dirt road.

I don't know how the pastor explained the turn of events to his flock. Perhaps they were so grateful for the reprieve that no one bothered to question it. But what surprised me at the time was that the next Sunday the church was as full as if nothing had ever happened.

When I pointed out to a young friend whose family was a part of that sect that the pastor had obviously been wrong and The

End hadn't come, his response was, "It might have," and refused to talk further about it.

Far as I know, the pastor's reputation didn't suffer a bit. In fact, the next year they built a new and larger church.

You might as well as laugh.

Ed Smith has taught in schools all over Newfoundland, finally settling in Springdale where he and his wife, Marion, still live. He has been a high school principal, an assistant superintendent of education, and principal of a college campus in Springdale. Ed retired in 1996, just over two years before a car accident left him paralyzed from the shoulders down.

He began writing a humour column for the local newspaper in 1980. Other papers soon began running the column, so that today "The View from Here" appears in six papers and magazines. He has been nominated for the Stephen Leacock Award for humour, and has written for the *Toronto Star* and *Reader's Digest*.

In 2001, Ed prepared a series of short radio clips on life with quadriplegia which he wrote and presented on CBC radio. These earned him The Canadian Nurses' Association award for excellence in broadcasting, and an international Gabriel award for writing that "upholds and uplifts the human spirit." Ed has been recognized by the Atlantic Community Newspapers Association for "hilarious" material. Four collections of his columns have also been published.

His Canadian Best-Selling *From the Ashes of My Dreams* is the winner of the 2003 Newfoundland and Labrador Book Award for non-fiction.

Ed Smith and his wife have four children and six grandchildren.

## *Also by Ed Smith*

Published in 2002, the critically acclaimed *From the Ashes of My Dreams* quickly became a Canadian Best-Seller. In 2003 it won the Newfoundland and Labrador Book Award for Non-fiction.